MUSEUMS, THE PUBLIC AND ANTHROPOLOGY

RANCHI ANTHROPOLOGY SERIES

1. Process, Performance, and Pilgrimage: A Study in Comparative Symbology/ Victor Witter Turner
2. Development of Researches in Anthropology in India: Bihar–A Case Study/ L.P. Vidyarthi and V.S. Upadhyay
3. Nature-Man-Spirit Complex in Tribal India/ R.S. Mann and Vijay S. Sahay (Eds.)
4. Microevolution/ B.M. Das
5. Tribal Festivals of Bihar: A Functional Analysis/ Ajit K. Singh
6. The Spectrum of the Sacred: Essays on the Religious Traditions of India/ Baidyanath Saraswati
7. Folklore: The Pulse of the People/ Mazharul Islam
8. Social Science and Indian Society: A Civilisational Perspective/ Baidya Nath Varma
9. Museums, the Public and Anthropology/ Michael M. Ames

About the Author

MICHAEL M. AMES is a well-known Canadian anthropologist who has conducted field work among the native Indians of the Northwest Coast of Canada, for more than two years in Sri Lanka, and for a year in India. Since 1975 he has served as professor and director of the University of British Columbia Museum of Anthropology, Vancouver, which has gained international attention for its pioneering work in museum techniques and for the quality of its educational programmes.

He has published on Buddhism and social change in Sri Lanka, the impact of industrialization on the Indian family system, the arts of acculturation, museum techniques, and the anthropology of anthropology. His current interests include the study of the democratization of cultural organizations and the social sciences in developed and developing societies, for which *Museums, The Public and Anthropology* is a first report.

Dr. Ames is a member of a number of international learned societies, national societies in Canada, India and the United States, and is a Fellow of the Royal Society of Canada.

RANCHI ANTHROPOLOGY SERIES-9

Gen. Editor : L.P. VIDYARTHI

MUSEUMS, THE PUBLIC AND ANTHROPOLOGY

A Study in the Anthropology of Anthropology

Michael M. Ames

UNIVERSITY OF BRITISH COLUMBIA PRESS,
VANCOUVER
and
CONCEPT PUBLISHING COMPANY PVT. LTD.
NEW DELHI-110059

International Standard Book Number
(UBC Press edition) 0-7748-0213-8

ISBN: 978-81-7022-125-8

Edition 2025

Published and Printed by

Concept
Since 1974

Concept Publishing Company Pvt. Ltd.
A/15-16, Commercial Block, Mohan Garden,
New Delhi-110059 (India)
T : 91-11-41101460
E : publishing@conceptpub.com, *W*: www.conceptpub.com

General Editor's Introduction

The Department of Anthropology of Ranchi University celebrated its Silver Jubilee in 1978. Again, it received the recognition of being the only U.G.C. Centre of Special Assistance in Anthropology in the country almost in the same year. During the tenure of my Presidentship of the International Union of Anthropological and Ethnological Sciences (1973-78) as well as Xth ICAES (1978), the Department was also called upon to perform several academic and professional roles involving it at the international level.

With this background, we ventured to launch a new series of publications entitled "Ranchi Anthropology Series" in the year 1980. This series is designed to provide a short but scholarly treatment of key problem-areas in anthropology. Under this series, in addition to lectures delivered at Ranchi by visiting scholars of national and international repute, we have also been publishing the theoretically oriented research work of local scholars as well as proceedings of national and international level seminars and symposia.

This book is the outcome of a series of six lectures delivered by Prof. Michael Ames in the years December 1983 – January 1984 during his stay at Ranchi. In recognition of his valuable contribution to the cause and study of social anthropology he was invited by the Indian Science Congress Association for its Ranchi conference which the late Prime Minister, Mrs. Indira Gandhi inaugurated. Incidentally, it turned out to be her last inaugural address to this august assembly of scholars and academics.

When Prof. Ames visited Ranchi during this period he was the guest of the Department of Special Assistance in the Department of Anthropology, Ranchi University. The talks he delivered are being reproduced in the shape of this book.

In the series of chapters Prof. Ames, an specialist in Museum methods, dwells systematically and at length on the rise of museums in the western world and their links with the anthropological development. As he authoritatively asserts he looks at the anthropological museum as artefacts of society, as exhibits in their own right, to see what can be learned about them, and through them, about ourselves. Thus the Museum is both a window and a looking glass.

It is for the first time that Prof. Ames in the light of modern development of museology and anthropology brings out the inter-relatedness of the Museum and the people and how the Museum can better serve the public interest. He has discussed pragmatically the role of the cultural centre in an urban setting for an overall material, cultural and recreational development. The development of such centres in the urban and/or industrial areas may play a constructive role in enriching the lifestyle of the people.

Prof. Ames, an eminent scholar of Indian anthropology and the Director of the Museum at the University of British Columbia, has done a valuable service to anthropology in general and Indian anthropology in particular by delivering the series of talks on our request and given us such a remarkable manuscript, meticulously prepared and carefully edited, for wider readership of the specialists and enlightened laymen.

Director,
Centre of Advanced Study in Anthropology
Ranchi University
RANCHI-834001 (India)

L.P. VIDYARTHI

Contents

Preface

Anthropology museums provide windows on other cultures of the world, but when they are examined more closely they can also be seen to mirror the profession of anthropology itself, both its achievements and its foibles. In the series of essays that follow I try to explore in a modest way museums both as window and as looking glass to see what can be discovered about museums and about the anthropological profession. The focus is on the situation in North America, and particularly Canada, since that is what is most familiar to me. Perhaps the examples given here will help to raise more general questions and to encourage others to broaden the comparative base.

Both museums and the profession of anthropology, it is suggested, are in jeopardy and need to be reformed if they are to play useful roles in contemporary democratic society; indeed, anthropology, at least, likely will have to change if it is even to survive. The major force for change considered is the process of democratization, which has been an integral part of the modernization of societies. What happens to museums and to the profession of anthropology when they are themselves confronted with the democratic idea, that revolutionary populist notion that ordinary people—"the public"—have a right to free access to knowledge and to its use, is the question asked.

The first chapter sets the problem within the historical context of the growth of public museums in the western world. Chapters 2 to 6 explore specific issues relating to museums and anthropology, while Chapter 7 returns to the beginning by asking once again whether museums and anthropology, at least as they are presently constituted in North America, have a useful future—or are their traditional privileges too much in peril. I am concerned throughout with the purposes museums and anthropology do and might serve. An equally important problem is the unsatisfactory state of theory and method in anthropology, but there is opportunity in these essays to make only a few casual observations, for example in Chapters 3. 4 and 5.

These essays are the result of some eight years of administration, teaching and reflection at the University of British Columbia Museum of

Anthropology, where I have had the privilege of serving as director since 1975. I have borrowed liberally from the works and ideas of others and am deeply grateful to them. Any merit found herein derives from their contributions, which I am passing on, while the errors, omissions, and distortions are my own inventions. I especially want to acknowledge the following individuals and institutions, because without their counsel or assistance the essays would not have reached this stage.

I thank Dr. L.P. Vidyarthi, a scholar of international repute and Head of the Department of Anthropology at Ranchi University, who kindly invited me to prepare these essays for presentation to his department and to the LXXI Indian Science Congress, which met at Ranchi in January 1984. I was honoured to be a guest both of the Congress and of the Ranchi Department of Anthropology during January, and was able to complete the material for publication during that visit. I also learned a good deal about Indian anthropology at the same time and how much it can teach the west about how scholarship can better serve the public interest.

Only Chapter 5 was previously published, though earlier versions of Chapters 3, 4 and 6 were presented to various learned societies in Canada and England; Chapter 4 is published in the Proceedings of the Royal Society of Canada, and Chapter 6 is to be published in the UNESCO Journal *Museum*. They are now published together under Dr. Vidyarthi's editorship. I am grateful that through his intervention this study of North American museums and anthropology should be published first in India since it, in a sense, completes a personal circle begun when I first published in North America research earlier conducted in South Asia (Sri Lanka in 1958-59, 1963 and India in 1967-68).

I am also grateful for the wide-ranging discussions with the faculty and students at Ranchi University, which helped to push my own thinking further along. It is clear that a new kind of museum is needed, one that can respond more effectively and more creatively to contemporary problems and opportunities, not only in developing nations like India but also in the so-called developed world of the west. This calls for a new kind of anthropologist as well. The traditional museum, with its elaborate and expensive exhibit constructions resembling little more than purified or genteel versions of Disneyland, is still very much in vogue, however, even though it is becoming evident that such museums serve a limited purpose and a limited clientele (the higher educated strata). Though ostensibly designed to serve the public, these large museums, it seems to me, are a more accurate reflection of the interests and aspirations of the museum profession. Yet it is difficult to think outside of this standard or mainstream model or to break from it without discarding the word "museum" itself. and perhaps that is what is required. The problem with museums is that they are called museums, and thus they automatically predetermine their mandate.

The Kwagiutl U'Mista Cultural Society in British Columbia, representing a number of Kwagiutl Indian tribes, calls its institution a "cultural centre" rather than a museum, though it preserves and exhibits artefacts along with promoting other cultural activities. We reached a similar conclusion in our deliberations at Ranchi in response to the question, "What kind of museum does a developing country like India need?" India could use museums of all types, of course, if it could afford the luxury: but the one that seemed to attract the most interest was the idea of a "Cultural Centre of Traditional and Contemporary Performing and Visual Arts," borrowing from the anthropological notions ot sacred complex, cultural performance, action anthropology, and museum ethnology. Anthropologists, with their holistic approach to society and culture, should be ideally suited to initiate and manage such cultural complexes that could assist in the promotion and regeneration of culture, especially for people whose own ways of living are subjected to risk because of rapid change, dislocation, domination or exploitation. Preserving the past is certainly important, but rather than simply being "mausoleums" of the past (even if Disnified ones), cultural centres could work more effectively, and their anthropologists more energetically, to make the past more relevant to people today, and to enhance the quality of life today. Such a new direction would be an ambitious undertaking, and difficult to achieve where vested interests in the standard model are strong. Perhaps, therefore, we need to look to minorities, indigenous groups, small communities, and to developing nations for creative innovations. That, at least, was the conclusion I reached at Ranchi.

The writings of George Appell, Nelson Graburn, Harry B. Hawthorn, Audrey Hawthorn, Tom McFeat, Milton Singer, William Sturtevant, and Wilcomb Washburn had a considerable influence on my outlook on museums, and I am pleased to use this occasion to record my appreciation.

I also benefited from numerous discussions with the officers of the Museums Assistance Programme of the National Museums of Canada, with the anthropologists in Canada's National Museum of Man, and with designers David Jensen and Rudy Kovach.

I am grateful to students at the University of British Columbia Museum of Anthropology, whose interest in and critical response to my teaching provoked me to think even harder. And I am especially indebted to my colleagues at the Museum of Anthropology—staff, volunteers, and students—for their patience, encouragement and inspiration as we together tried to work through many of the ideas and problems discussed here while somehow also managing to operate a busy and "democratized" museum-as-a-cultural-centre. Thanks are also due to Sandra Hawkes for he editorial assistance, and Lucie Dufresne for preparing the index.

Acknowledgement is made to the Canadian Museums Association, the University of British Columbia Social Science and Humanities Research Grant Committee and the Dean of the Faculty of Arts, and the Social Sciences and Humanities Research Council of Canada for travel and research grants that supported earlier stages of the work represented in these essays, and to the Social Sciences and Humanities Research Council for a leave fellowship (1983-84) that gave me the quiet space in which to prepare the material for presentation to Ranchi University and for publication.

I thank the Canadian Ethnology Society, the Committees on Museum Ethnology and Architecture and Museum Techniques of the International Council of Museums, the Royal Society of Canada, and the International Congress of Anthropological and Ethnological Sciences for opportunities to present earlier versions of several of these essays.

Finally, and most important of all, I express special gratitude to my family for kindly bearing with me and without me these many years.

Ranchi and Vancouver
January 1984

Michael M. Ames

1

The Development of Museums in the Western World

Tensions Between Democratization and Professionalization [1]

It has been said that once upon a time the Welsh poet Dylan Thomas walked into the museum in his home town and looked at the stuffed animals crowded into their dusty cases with faded labels. "This museum," he observed, "ought to be in a museum!" (Morris 1983:1).

My purpose in this series of lectures is to go beyond Dylan Thomas and to subject to critical scrutiny all museums, both the new as well as the antiquated ones, those venerable institutions designed, as one sage put it (Welch 1983: 61), for "useful and curious learning." I want to look at museums as artefacts of society, as exhibits in their own right, to see what can be learned about them, and through them, about ourselves. My focus will be upon museums of anthropology in Europe and North America, since I am more familiar with them. Their ostensible purpose is to provide windows on the other cultures of the world, but upon examination we will discover that they mirror as well the profession of anthropology itself and its socio-cultural context. I will look at the anthropology museum in the western world as both window and looking glass to see what can be learned about museums and anthropology and their uncertain futures. The essays are presented as exercises in the social anthropology of museums and anthropology.

The first task is to consider how modern western museums of anthropology came to be what they are, how they formed part of the general evolution of museums in the western world. I will limit myself to only a few incidents in the recent history of museums, and refer to only a few examples. My purpose is not to provide a detailed history but to outline a general process and to speculate about the implications of that process. Since the history of anthropology museums is part of a larger social movement, it will be necessary at times to refer to museums of history, art and science as well. They share the same evolutionary path, though my primary interest is in the consequences for anthropology and how it is practiced.

My historical overview will be incomplete in several other ways as well, for I will not consider such museum-like institutions as fairs, sideshows, circuses, zoos and church and temple reliquaries; nor can I consider the history of museums outside Europe and North America. Both my time and my knowledge are too limited to attempt such important tasks.

There are nevertheless still some useful things that can be said about my circumscribed topic, the development in the West of museums that deal with the history and works of humankind. Their evolution parallels in important ways the growth of scholarship since the Renaissance and the concomitant growth of the revolutionary idea that people have both a need and a right to learn freely and to have free access to knowledge. These developments are all part of an overall trend towards increased democratization. What happens to museums and those who work in them as they become progressively, even if at times begrudgingly, democratized is what I want to consider in this chapter.

A few hundred years ago in European countries scholarship and museum collections were restricted to a few people, typically only members of the ruling classes or gentry. Public access to writings and works of art was strictly limited to distant viewing in formal institutions like cathedrals or on formal royal occasions. Scholarly work on museum collections was insignificant, for private access was granted only through the favour of the owner, and there was neither the necessity nor the means of communicating knowledge beyond the privileged few.

Many collections of natural and cultural materials began as private trophies, curiosities, and booty of the wealthy; other collections were religiously inspired and were used by the churches more for veneration than for study.

The Renaissance brought expansion and intensification of scholarly activity along with the growth of the middle classes, while the growing European exploration of the rest of the world contributed to the accumulation of treasures and souvenirs gathered from all over. As the collections grew in size and complexity, so did the need to house and care for them, and, therefore, also the need for people who specialized in the care and management of collections.

The invention of the printing press, the spread of education in vernacular languages, the increasing importance of the middle classes, and the development of political democracy all contributed to a wider distribution of knowledge. The movement to cities brought about by the industrial revolution encouraged various forms of popular expression and also the recognition of the need for social reforms and more accessible education. It was in this context of change and growth that large private collections shifted into public or government ownership, and museums began to open to the general public.

The earliest public museums established in Western Europe, during the eighteenth and nineteenth centuries, owed much to the already existing collections that were in private hands. On the continent, "the Cabinets of Curiosities" held by royalty were especially important; in England, private collections of scientists and travellers, who were guided to some degree in their collecting by a plan of research or by a certain set of ideas, played the larger role (Frese 1960 : 6).

Some of the European royal cabinets were of considerable age. They were founded to house the exotic tributes, such as rare and precious gifts received from foreign ambassadors and other goods royalty seized as their natural right. These various objects illustrated the world-wide powers and interests of the reigning monarch or prince and his dynasty. Many of the ethnographic objects in the great Musee de l' Homme in Paris, for example, came from French royal collections. The Cabinet of Curiosities of the Danish kings led to the National Museum at Copenhagen. The collections of the Electors of Brandenburg and Kings of Prussia formed the nucleus of the Berlin ethnographic museum, and so on (Frese 1960 : 7).

When museums took over royal collections they also took on a number of the royal functions; such as the protection they offered learning, the safety and continuity provided the collections themselves, and the "symbolic function of being a national treasury or shrine" (Frese 1960 : 8). There was another function or role museums added, "one of the essential aspects of the change in the first half of the nineteenth century from cabinets of curiosities to museums," which was the introduction of systems of scientific classification and interpretation of artefacts (ibid.). With the emergence of public museums we find also the emergence of a museum profession.

With some exceptions, especially regarding the scholarly collections in England and Europe, many of the early cabinets of curiosities were until the middle of the nineteenth century haphazardly organized and managed, a jumble of the quaint and the curious. The gradual incorporation of collections into museums with their own facilities and full-time staff to care for them led to a different way of handling and interpreting the collections. What were objects of curiosity or glory became scientific specimens, and scholars devoted themselves to their study and classification. Collections were organized and grouped according to what at the time were thought to be universal themes, such as race or evolutionary stage. The keepers of these nineteenth century public museums considered their scientific work of such pressing importance, in fact, that it was still some time before the public was actually granted much access. But access was eventually granted, and once it was it could only increase, and it would appear that over the next hundred years as public attendance grew, scholarly work would seem to decline. The purpose of specimen classification also appeared to change, from serving the interests of the scientist to serving the needs of popular education. And in those changes lie the source of many problems.

A concrete example would be useful at this point. Consider the origins of one of the great museums in the world, the British Museum in London.[2]

Three major collections owned by English notables provided the foundation for the British Museum.

In 1753 a physician and botanist, Sir Hans Sloane, bequeathed his extensive collection of botanical, geological, and zoological specimens to the British nation, on condition that 20,000 pounds be paid to his family, "desiring very much that these things, tending many ways to the manifestation of the glory of God, the confutation of atheism and its consequences, the use and improvement of the arts and sciences, and benefit of mankind, may remain together and not be separated."

This bequest apparently served to speed up legislation for a national repository to house this and other collections which the Crown was acquiring, including especially the library of Sir Robert Cotton.

The Cotton library was not actually bequeathed to the Crown but seized by it, on suspicion that certain manuscripts of a seditious nature had been deliberately placed there by its owner. Whether this was true or not, the government apparently thought that most of the books were worth keeping anyway. Also, around this time the Countess of Oxford decided to sell to the government the library and antiquities of Robert Harley, the first Earl of Oxford, for 30,000 pounds.

These offers, along with other events, led to the establishment of the British Museum. It opened to the public in 1759, and in 1781 the Royal Society turned over its entire collection to the trustees of the British Museum. Establishing a national museum to house major collections is one thing; making those collections accessible to the public is quite another matter, however, and that took much longer to bring about.

At first it was felt that only the desirable public should be admitted to the museum. As Henry remarks (1911, quoted in Key 1973 : 36) in his history of the British Museum, "it demanded something like a mathematical calculation to determine when the building was and was not open." For example:

> 'except Saturday and Sunday in each week; likewise except Christmas Day and one week after...also except the week after Easter and the week after Whit Sunday and except Good Friday and all days which are now, or shall hereafter be specially appointed Thanksgivings or fasts by public authority.' Then followed a further reminder that 'Between the months of September and April inclusive, from Monday to Friday the museum be opened from nine o'clock till three and likewise at the same hours on Tuesday, Wednesday and Thursday in May, June, July and August but on Monday and Friday only from one o'clock to eight in the afternoon.'

After figuring out the timetable, the visitor was advised that no more than ten people could be admitted at any one time, and that they would be escorted around in groups for a thirty minute tour. To sign on, Archie Key (1973 : 36-37) reports in his history of museums,

> personal application was made to the porter at his lodge who inscribed in the register the name, condition (drunk, sober, clean, dirty, seemingly of means or otherwise) after which the librarian or his understudy decided whether the applicant was "proper" for admission, "and until...the solution being in the affirmative...either of those officials issued an invitation, the prospective visitor had no more chance of getting inside the museum than Satan has of eluding the vigilance of St. Peter."

The British Museum was not the only institution that had to contend with visitors. The first public museum in England was Oxford's Ashmolean, which opened its doors in 1683 (MacGregor 1983a : 97). When the German scholar Zacharias Conrad von Uffenbach visited the Ashmolean in 1710, he had serious reservations both about the quality of people granted admission and the way the custodians cared for their collections. As he later recorded in his diary (Welch 1983 : 62):

> The specimens in the museum might also be much better arranged and preserved, although they are better kept than those in Gresham College, London, which are far too bad considering their splendid

description. But it is surprising that things can be preserved even as well as they are, since the people impetuously handle everything in the usual English fashion and, as I mentioned before, even the women are allowed up here for sixpence; they run here and there, grabbing at everything and taking no rebuff from the *Sub-custos* (deputy keeper).

In 1773 an evidently exasperated owner of a private museum inserted the following notice in a London newspaper (Bogaart 1978 : 43):

> This is to inform the public that being tired out with the insolence of the common people who I have hitherto indulged with a sight of my museum, I am now come to the resolution of refusing admittance to the lower class except they come provided with a ticket from some gentleman or lady of my acquaintance.

In the 1700s it would require several visits to obtain an admission ticket to the British Museum, and a third visit to actually gain entry (Key 1973: 37). Regulations were gradually relaxed over the years, but only slowly. Even in 1882, 123 years after the museum first opened to the public, it still took determination and perseverance. As one man noted (ibid.), after waiting two weeks for his tickets,

> It was the room, the glass cases, the shelves which I saw; not the museum itself, so rapidly were we hurried through the departments...In about thirty minutes we finished our silent journey through this princely mansion, which would have well taken thirty days. I went out much about as wise as I went in, but with the severe reflection that, for fear of losing my chance, I had that morning abruptly torn myself from three gentlemen with whom I was engaged in an interesting conversation, had lost my breakfast, got wet to the skin, spent half a crown in coach, paid two shillings for a ticket, and had been hackneyed through the rooms with violence.

National museums gradually introduced more liberal policies towards admissions as they became progressively more involved in the social and political developments of the eighteenth and nineteenth centuries. Educational and welfare reforms called for more services to the working classes, and that included opening the doors of museums and other educational institutions. This democratization of museums had important repercussions for the philosophy of the museum enterprise and for the public role of museums, something which Duncan Cameron (1971) has pointed to in his widely quoted paper, "The museum, a temple or the forum".

Collections held in private ownership, Cameron said (1971: 15), made private or personal statements about the owners:

> The collections may have said, 'Look how curious I am and how meticulous and how thorough. Here is my scientific collection, which reaffirms my belief in the order of the universe and the laws of nature.' The collection may have said, 'See how rich I am,' or, 'Look at this. Look at how I surround myself with beautiful things. See what good taste I have, how civilized and cultivated I am.' It may have said, 'Oh! I am a man of the world who has travelled much. Look at all the places I have been. Look at all the mysterious things I have brought back from my adventures. Yes! I am an adventurer.'

When others viewed a private collection they were not expected to identify with it, to see it as *their* collection; nor were they expected to accept the collector's view of the world or of himself. It was understood that the collection represented a personal statement, a personal possession.

The transfer of private collections to public hands and the introduction of the idea that the public should have access to these collections brought about a significant shift in how people interpreted the meaning of those collections. They were no longer considered a private matter. In declaring these collections to be publicly owned, Cameron states (1971: 16):

> it was no longer being said that this was someone else's collection that you, the visitor, could look at. Rather, it was being said that this was *your* collection and therefore it should be meaningful to *you*, the visitor.

The granting of public access therefore also entailed the granting of a degree of public control over the museum enterprise, the purpose of the institution and the collections it contained. This control was founded on the expectation that publicly owned collections would be made meaningful to that public. Thus, gradually, the public—or more correctly, the educated classes—came to believe that they had the right to expect that the collections would present and interpret the world in some way consistent with the values they held to be good, with the collective representations they held to be appropriate, and with the view of social reality they held to be true.

These values, collective representations and models of social reality reflected the interests of the educated classes, of course, those people who, since the beginning and to this day, control and patronize the great museums of the world. Museums are products of the establishment and represent the assumptions and definitions of that establishment, just as do most other major institutional complexes in large-scale societies. That is hardly surprising, nor is it unusual that most members of the educated classes assume that their view represents the proper view for society as a whole. The museum becomes a temple for the society that sustains it (Cameron 1971: 17):

> ...those segments of society with the power to do so...created museums that were the temples within which they enshrined those things they held to be significant and valuable. The public generally accepted the idea that if it was in the museum, it was not only real but represented a standard of excellence. If the museum said that this and that was so, then that was a statement of truth.

The museum is where you would go to compare your own private perceptions of reality with what was the accepted and approved, and therefore "objective," view of reality, enshrined within the museum.

Before the advent of publicly owned museums, to summarize, large collections were the personal property of the wealthy, the royalty, and a few scholars, and these collections were used, by and large, to further personal interest and personal definitions of value and social reality. Visitors, on those rare and special occasions they were permitted to view these private collections, were not expecting that what they saw would be meaningful to them in a direct and personal sense. Collections were interesting "curiosities".

The nationalization of major collections leading to the establishment of national or publicly owned museums meant the nationalization of image-making as well. Museums now "owned" by the public also became responsible for reflecting and promoting the public's definition of truth and value. For this reason, Cameron says (1971: 17), the museum became closer in function to the church than to the school:

> The museum provides opportunity for reaffirmation of the faith; it is a place for private and intimate experience, although it is shared with many others; it is, in concept, the temple of the muses where today's personal experience of life can be viewed in the context of 'The Works of God Through All the Ages; the Arts of Man Through All the Years'.[3]

The great museum of today is equivalent to the cathedral of the Middle

Ages, the palace of the eighteenth century, and the Eiffel Tower in the nineteenth century: it expresses in a modern idiom—both in its architecture and its content—the essential values and world view of a community, and through this expression it authenticates (Meyer 1979: 130).

The museum as a publicly owned civic temple is the culmination of several centuries of development. Personal collections and private museums existed for centuries, and continue. Religiously oriented relic chambers, ornamented cathedrals and temples, and monuments also have long histories. But publicly owned and publicly accessible museums identifying with the state or the nation in a secular rather than religious sense, expressing and authenticating established views, are a new phenomenon, probably no more than a hundred to two hundred years old.

A large public museum may express and authenticate the established or official values and images of a society in several ways, *directly,* by promoting and affirming the dominant values, and *indirectly,* by subordinating or rejecting alternate values. A work of art that never gets hung in major art galleries is art that is likely to be forgotten. Images and records that are relegated to the closed storerooms of a museum are relegated to obscurity.

Sociologist Dean MacCannell, in his provocative book on the Tourist (1976), highlights this double role of affirmation and subordination played by modern museums. The idea of the modern museum, he says (1976: 84), is to contribute to the unification of society by exercising control over both tradition and nature, subordinating both to modernity. Museums put nature and culture in their proper places, under glass in display cases, and, therefore, under control. MacCannell says that in this sense museums are both "anti-historical" and "unnatural".

They are not anti-historical and unnatural in the sense of being opposed to history and nature, but in that they *control* and *subordinate* both to contemporary definitions of social reality. Museums preserve history and nature by taming them both, subjecting them to the technical control of the designers and fabricators and the conceptual control of the curators. As museums preserve, MacCannell continues, "they automatically separate modernity from its past and from nature and elevate it above them." Nature, the past, and traditional societies are made a part of the present, not as things of equal value with the present, but as "tourist attractions".

Museums place history, nature, and traditional societies under glass, in artificially constructed dioramas and tableaux, thus sanitizing, insulating, plasticizing and preserving them as attractions and simple lesson aids; by virtue of their location, they are implicity compared with and subordinated to contemporary established values and definitions of social reality. When we "museumify" other cultures and our own past, we exercise a conceptual control over them; and when this museumification process involves high technology—elaborate dioramas, life-sized reproductions of actual settings, and complex audio-visual aids–we are demonstrating and exhibiting the superiority of our technology (Halpin 1978). There is a museum in Canada that has installed in its anthropology gallery one of the finest fishing scenes I have seen anywhere. It is complete and accurate down to the smallest detail, with carefully fabricated replicas of fish and plant life shown underwater, and with fish hooks and nets hanging down from above to demonstrate how the aborigines used to fish. It is reported by one of the curators that the most frequently asked question by the public does not concern the Indians or the fish, but how the designers were able to construct such a realistic scene. Though the Indians were apparently clever fishermen, they obviously did not compare with the wonders of modern museum technology.

The museum as it has developed into the twentieth century, especially in North America, has become something like a public temple, an institution that plays an important role in expressing and authenticating established values and images of society (Cameron) and in affirming the subordination of other values and images (MacCannell). The large civic or national museum of history or art is treated by the public as a standard and an authority on history and culture and as a custodian of the socially approved definitions of social reality, principally those definitions representing the interests of the educated classes.

During the past twenty years or so, however, the process of democratization that began several centuries before has continued to work towards an ever broadening definition of those who are to be included in the process. The definition of the "public" that is to be served by museums expands accordingly, to include such categories as school children, the working classes, minorities, and the handicapped. But there is another twist to the story. Today, democratization of museums not only means extending access to a wider range of people, but entails as well the obligation to *work to make the people come.* Museums are now expected to actively and energetically seek a broader audience, and to please them as well. Increasing attendance figures and high public profile have become the two most common factors used to rate the success of museums.

This further extension of the democratic principle, which obliges museums to make themselves increasingly attractive to the general public, greatly affects their organization and operation. Just as in the nineteenth century the granting of limited public access to national museums entailed granting a degree of public control over the museum enterprise, so today the granting of popular access also entails a further extension of public control. Museums are now expected to present an image of social reality and to promote a set of values that will appeal to the masses while also remaining within what the establishment would consider to be appropriate limits. The inner workings of museums are changed accordingly. Rather than museums existing for the purpose of preserving and studying collections, museums and collections, especially in North America, at least, now exist more and more for the purpose of serving the public. This changing emphasis, a logical extension of a process begun many decades earlier, has profound implications for the social organization of museums and for the conditions of work within them. What this means for anthropologists who work in and around museums, and what it means for the future of both anthropology and museums, are matters I would next like to consider.

NOTES

1. This chapter was first presented as a Special Lecture to Section 8: Anthropology and Archaeology, LXXI Indian Science Congress, Ranchi, 4 January 1984.

2. Most of the information for this account was drawn from Key 1973: 36-38.

3. Text of the inscription on the front of the Royal Ontario Museum, Toronto, Canada.

2

Dilemmas of the Practical Anthropologist

Public Service versus Professional Interests[1]

It is an honourable tradition in anthropology to talk about general issues on the basis of particular field studies, and that is what I will attempt here. I am interested in the dilemmas that confront anthropologists in contemporary society, especially those produced by the continuing growth of social and political democracy. One democratic belief that is especially interesting is the idea that the general public has a right to share in and benefit from knowledge produced by scholars (Manning 1983b: 5). How are anthropologists responding to this expectation?

Following the anthropological tradition, I will explore this general issue through the idiosyncrasies of a single case. I will not cover all anthropology, which is too broad a topic for me to handle. Instead, I will limit myself to the socio-cultural branch, which I will refer to, following the museum custom, as "ethnology", and within that category I will focus on those ethnologists associated with museums in North America, and particularly in Canada. Like Malinowski and his Trobrianders, Firth and his Tikopeans, Rivers and his Toda, and Seligman and his Veddah, though I am afraid with considerably less skill, I offer my study of an exotic tribe of North American museum ethnologists as a comment upon a general issue that should concern us all. I will even suggest that my tribe, for many years now a neglected and unstudied part of anthropology—a "weaker section", as it were—may be, in fact, a bellwether for the future of the discipline.

I begin my field report with a brief comment on the culture history of North American museums. Around the middle of the last century two institutions were established in the United States that represented successful and dramatically contrasting ideas of what a museum should be. Each of these ideas would have a different set of consequences for people working in museums.

One of those nineteenth century institutions was the "National Museum of the United States," subsequently known as the Smithsonian National Museum of Natural History, which came into being in the American capital of Washington during the 1850s as a result of a bequest from the Englishman James Smithson. Another important institution to emerge around that time was the "American Museum" in New York City, which the famous American entrepreneur Phineas T. Barnum purchased in 1841. Barnum's museum burnt to the ground in July 1865, while the Smithsonian went on to become one of the world's great museums; yet both made important contributions to the public understanding of museums, and their contrast in styles reflects one of the major dilemmas North American museums, and those working within them, face today.

The Smithsonian was established, in accordance with Smithson's original bequest, "for the increase and diffusion of knowledge among men" (Kopper 1982: 37), and it represents today the classical model of a distinguished museum, with its seven disciplinary departments representing the biological, anthropological, and earth sciences, and its scientific collections of over 60 million specimens ranging from the famous Hope Diamond that came from the Indian subcontinent, four million plant specimens, 26 million insects, 34,146 nests and eggs, several tons of meteorite fragments, over 20,000 human skulls, numerous ethnological items, 14 million postage stamps, and even, so it has been said, the ashes of a deceased staff member and his first wife and the pickled brains of two former curators (Bonner 1981; Kopper 1982: 26, 53-54; Smithsonian Institution 1977). The museum has maintained since its early days active programmes of collecting, research, scientific publication, and public education.

Barnum, on the other hand, bought the American Museum in New York as a business venture. His intent was profit, not education or moral uplift, and he

> pursued any feature or oddity that might attract customers. Advertisement and display rather than scholarship and comprehensiveness were his strong suits (Harris 1981: 56).

Barnum's collections, though smaller in size than the Smithsonian's, certainly competed for variety. He acquired numerous "curiosities and performers" including three serpents fed noonday meals before the public, two whales that swam in a tank of salt water, a white elephant, hippos, bears, wolves, a herd of American buffalo, waxwork figures, midgets, dwarfs, giants, bearded ladies, fat boys, rope dancers, jugglers, performing American Indians, a tattooed man, gypsy girls, albinos, and a group of "industrious fleas" (Alexander 1979: 49-50; Harris 1981:40; Wallace 1959).

While the Smithsonian concerned itself with scholarship, Barnum emphasized showmanship. He decorated the exterior of his museum building with brightly coloured banners advertising the wonders of the world to be seen within, installed spotlights on the roof, a musical band on the exterior balcony, and lectures, performances and plays inside (Harris 1981 : 54). He also advertised widely and cleverly manipulated the local press to his advantage. The Smithsonian, not surprisingly, was more conservative in its actions and operated on public funds appropriated by the United States Congress. Barnum operated his museum at a profit earned from admission fees.

Barnum's American Museum in New York, though shortlived, became the most popular institution of its kind in the country, and though it and others like it were condemned for their vulgarization—"a mere place of popular amusement," scoffed one learned critic in 1851 (Harris 1981: 33)—they catered to a general public whose interests were being expanded by the growth of the democratic spirit in America. Following the American Revolution, 1775 to 1783, there were increasing public proclamations that all authority—social, moral, aesthetic, and religious—should ultimately rest "in the hearts and minds of the ordinary citizen, the much-celebrated common man" (Harris 1981: 3). Barnum was fully conscious of this new democratic sensibility, "and he appealed directly to its vanities and deceits" (ibid., p. 4). In contrast to the dignified image of the British Museum, with its tediously catalogued treasures of art and science and its erudite programmes of research and instruction, which was at that time promoted as the index of civilization, the Barnum type of museum was little more than, in the caustic words of our 1851 critic (Harris 1981: 3, 310), ' a place for some stuffed birds and animals, for the exhibition of monsters, and for vulgar dramatic performances."

North American museums, and those working within them, have struggled ever since with this challenge: can they be serious and popular at the same time; can they retain their scholarly credentials while catering to untutored public interests? Can an institution be both Smithsonian and Barnum? The dilemma, cast in these terms, seems extreme; but in keeping with the tradition of anthropological case studies, an exaggerated example may serve to highlight the problems that result when the privileges of scholarship are confronted by the growth of the democratic spirit.

Barnum's museum burnt to the ground 24 years after he acquired it, but the ideal of a museum that can be successful by serving public interests continues. And the attempt by museums to fulfil this idea creates incredible stresses and strains for those who work within them, including, of course, ethnologists who strive to be both professionals and public servants at the same time. To understand the nature of these pressures it will be useful to explore more fully the two models I have introduced, of the distinguished scholarly museum on the one hand, and of the blatantly popular museum on the other. Taking the scholarly institution first, we can say that its purposes are at least two: "first, to provide a source for scientific research and secona to stimulate the public interest, by exhibitions and other means, in the results of these researches" (Washburn 1961:192, quoting from the handbook of Sweden's Nordiska Museum). According to Smithsonian scholar Wilcomb Washburn (ibid.), the traditional American definition of "museum" says that a museum is intended to educate, promote research, and preserve cultural heritage; but that, he says, is not enough:

> It is not enough...to give three cheers for research, education, and preservation, as the great functional trinity of the museum. In a great museum, as in a great university, research into the unknown must be the passion which dominates all and on which the functions of conservation and education depend.

"I do not hesitate to say," Franz Boas said in his 1907 paper on museum administration, "that the essential justification for the maintenance of large museums lies wholly in their importance as necessary means for the advancement of Science" (Boas 1907: 929). The large museum, he continued, "is the only means of bringing together and of preserving intact large series of material which for all time to come must form the basis of scientific inductions." The purpose of the museum, in the proverbial nutshell, is "to serve the progress of science."

Paul Joseph Sachs, who for many years taught museum work at Harvard University's Fogg Museum, and trained generations of American museum workers, also emphasized the role of scholarship in the training of a curator. A proper curator, he said (Meyer 1979: 41), "must first and foremost be a broad, well-trained scholar, a linguist, and then in due course, a specialist, a scholar with wide bibliographic knowledge, a scholar with broad human sympathies including a belief in popular education, a curator and administrator...."

There is, on the other side, a view of museums that emphasizes their public functions. Barnum, to return to our extreme example, did not develop his museums (he operated two in New York City, a third in Philadelphia, and an aquarium in Boston) to increase knowledge or public enlightenment, but simply to make a profit by attracting the public (Harris 1981: 56). Governments today recognize that publicly operated museums cannot be expected to make a profit, but they *are* expected to give priority to serving public interests. Consider as one example the policy statement on museums issued in 1977 by the Government of Quebec, a provincial administration in Canada (Boucher 1977:54): "Museums should be perceived as vehicles for cultural promotion," the Quebec Minister of Culture stated, "while, at the same time, providing attractions, encounters, exchanges, and extension services." There is no mention of research here, nor in the list of priorities for museum development that the minister presented:

1. To assure the conservation of our cultural heritage;
2. to promote the relevance of collections through the development of the educational aspects of their presentation;
3. to assure their availability to the greatest possible number of Quebeckers; and
4. to transform museums and exhibition centres into culturally alive institutions.

The act of parliament which established the National Museum of Man in Canada also highlights the public role of the National Museum. Its purpose, the act states (Taylor 1982:5) is "to demonstrate...the works of man, with special but not exclusive reference to Canada, so as to promote interest therein throughout Canada and to disseminate knowledge thereof." In 1972, the Government of Canada announced a museums policy for all of Canada, the objectives of which were "to increase physical and intellectual access to our natural, cultural and technological heritage as represented in collections across Canada, and to ensure that these collections are preserved for the benefit of present and future generations".

These government agencies are not calling for a Barnum museum of curiosities, with its bearded ladies, dwarfs, performing whales, and industrious fleas—though, I dare say, some museums would benefit from more lively programming—but they are stating that museums have a primary obligation to be accessible to the public and to inform them in an entertaining manner. The public as the true owners should be true beneficiaries of public museums (Cameron 1982: 179). In response, museums have made energetic efforts to increase their service to wider publics. It is as if they were running popularity contests, Duncan Cameron, one of Canada's leading museum administrators, observed (ibid., p. 180):

> ...we desperately wanted to be popular. We wanted to be loved. And we were reacting to the voices of our masters—boards of governors, governments and their funding agencies—who wanted to see dramatic growth in attendance curves and some of whom saw us as in competition with zoos, Disneyland, the local country fair and Evel Knievel.[2]

Disneyland is today's version of the Barnum problem: how can a museum be as popular as Disneyland without actually becoming a Disneyland, an image—like Barnum's American Museum—guaranteed to make all upstanding museum people cringe. A good museum, it is now often said, with more longing than hope, should be "more than a Disneyland experience", which means it should avoid "flashy multi-media presentations" and other gimmicks, yet still provide lively educational messages that will appeal to mass audiences (Bruman 1982; Levine and Sears 1982). The goal, Jean Andre, one of Canada's top museum exhibit designers, recently observed, is (Freedman 1980):

> a nice balance between exciting visuals and swallowing the pill. We're not supposed to be Disneyland.

Few museums have worked more energetically to achieve a happy balance between mass public appeal and scholarly respectability than has the Smithsonian itself. While a few Smithsonian staff members may, as Philip Kopper put in this magnificent story of the Smithsonian (1982: 197), "look up from their microscopes and down their noses at what they call 'public entertainment'," the vast majority willingly accept the museum's public responsibility (ibid., pp. 191, 194):

> to diffuse knowledge broadly among people without regard to scientific background, intellectual origin or academic status. Many of the scientists do it daily as they freely offer advice to everyone from schoolchildren seeking grist for science reports to farmers fighting a new pest to bemused heirs hoping to name the pressed herbs in late

> Great Aunt Julia's treasured herbarium. Other scientists devote the greater part of their professional time for some years to the planning, design, and installation of an exhibit which may well last longer than they will. As one department chairman puts it, 'Any scientist who isn't interested in public education shouldn't be here.'

The public galleries of the Smithsonian are thus designed to appeal to the general public, "to accommodate—indeed to impress and edify and boggle—everyone who enters" (Kopper 1982: 191)

As museums become more oriented to public service through programmes of education and entertainment, however, opportunities for scholarly research appear to recede. This is at least the case for those institutions that cannot afford to maintain separate and insulated research divisions. A number of large public museums in Canada, for example, have ruled that research, other than for exhibitions, must be done on a curator's own personal time. The curator is trained in the university system where individual research is presented as the primary good, and is then placed in a work situation where the collective need to serve the public is given primacy. The dilemma for the curator is twofold: first, to seek status within one's own profession, ethnology in the case at hand, one must research and publish in scholarly journals, while to retain status within the museum one must also engage in public service; and second, to conduct scholarly research one must follow a pursuit that is typically individual and competitive, whereas to do museum work one participates in endeavours that are interdisciplinary and collaborative. The museum ethnologist is caught between what often appear to be rapidly diverging standards. This is the "curator's dilemma", a "conflict of interest between duties towards the collections and personal research, to say nothing of exhibits and meeting the visiting public (Fenton 1960: 335), a situation some (Squires 1969) more dramatically refer to as curatorial schizophrenia.

The curatorial function should have a high degree of professionalism associated with it, says Donald F. Squires (1969: 19), who was once deputy director of the Smithsonian Museum of Natural History; but curatorial work often "bogs down in service activities." Museums are increasingly populated by specialists trained in the image of the university professor, Squires continues (ibid., p. 20), who seek employment in museums because they believe, incorrectly, they will be more sheltered there. But once in the museum, says Squires (ibid.),

> the curator frequently finds that he is asked to pass judgment upon and participate in a bewildering variety of activities—lecturing to chil-

> dren's groups and adult members, preparing materials for grade and high school classes, writing popular articles and books, book prefaces and reviews, preparing, evaluating and pricing materials for museum shop sales, serving as moderator for a public that is acquiring materials and seeking to know their values and authenticity, providing long-range judgments of future needs of the scientist in his own and related disciplines and specialties in larger museums, supervising the maintenance of a large and often burdensome collection of objects, tending to the needs of his visiting associates, keeping up the new literature, and undertaking original research in his own speciality.

This "multiplicity of activities...forces the curatorial staff to adopt a corresponding 'multiple' view toward their careers," Squires concludes, "and this I believe is the nub of the problem causing schizophrenia of these museums" (ibid.).

There is a particularly good example of the curatorial plight that I would like to present as an illustration of the point being made here. Dr. Marie-Françoise Guédon is a young Canadian ethnologist who served for six years at Canada's National Museum of Man, before resigning to accept a professorial position in a Canadian university. She recently published an article (1983) commenting upon her years in the museum, entitled "A case of mistaken identity (the education of a naive museum ethnologist)." I quote from her article.

There are basic contradictions built into the role of museum curator, Guédon states: "...the impossibility of being at once a full-time researcher, a full-time administrator, a full-time curator, and a full-time exhibit specialist..." (1983: 253).

When she applied for the position of Ethnologist at the Museum of Man, she said she was attracted by the offer of field work as part of her duties (ibid., p. 254): "60% of my time to be spent on research, the presence of huge collections and the opportunity to be in contact with the public, with administrators and with colleagues." It was only after taking the position that Dr. Guédon learned to her regret that the job "was more than full-time."

> Let me say right away (she writes) that I had not counted on the administrative nature of the institution. I had to learn to cope with the multiple pressures of administrative duties, administrative personnel, and administrative restrictions. I had to learn, too, to be on the defensive all the time, since in terms of duties, division matters came before the research programme for which one was hired and which formed the reference for one's advancement and working level (ibid.).

Dr, Guedon continues:

> Let us face it, research does not have a good reputation in museums, no matter how praised by directors. It is of no use to administrators. So, unless one refuses to answer memos asking for reports, calculations, information, budgets, other items of no consequence, there is little time left for research (ibid.).

Dr. Guedon said that when she finally realized, after six years at the National Museum, that field work had become a privilege rather than a duty she was ready to leave the museum (1983: 255):

> By choice—and by calling—I am an ethnographer; I was turning into an administrator...a common complaint, none the less true since it had become a cliche. I was not strong enough to shut my door and work in, rather than for, the museum.

The pressure of exhibit work was one of the deciding factors for Dr. Guedon (ibid.):

> Exhibits are the "raison d'etre" of museums, particularly anthropology museums. Anthropologists working for museums may know this, but it took the naive employee which I was several years to understand how exhibits were shaping my life and my career. I include here not only the work for temporary or permanent display open to the public, but also the work on related items; catalogues and popular publications, didactic collections of artefacts, and information sheets for schools and visitors, and so on.

Exhibits could be exciting work, she adds, but they are not because they are collective endeavours performed within an hierarchical organization that operates according to established standards and schedules. The intellectual freedom the individual scholarly entrepreneur has been taught to expect as a natural right does not prepare such a person for the kind of team work and public responsibility required in museums today.

Guedon contrasts the production of an exhibit with what is expected in academic circles (1983: 256-7), and I would like to repeat her comparison here in detail.

a. In a museum, one is instructed to present certain information for a given display or project which one very rarely chooses. (The academic usually generates his own subject).

b. The text is reviewed—which often means corrected, shortened, lengthened, or rewritten, by many different authors, including administrators, designers, and other exhibit specialists. (Imagine the uproar if the head of an anthropology department checked his faculty's papers before conferences.)

c. Any change in a text requires, of course, if not a change in design or artefacts or lettering, at least the signature of all supervisors...

d. Instead of writing for other specialists, one writes "for the public.' According to most guidelines, the public's intellectual level oscillates between ten and twelve years of age. So: "Use simple words," (do not introduce such terms as matrilineal, even with a definition). "Use short sentences." (Do not play with abstract concepts.) Everything one wants to convey has to be presented in statements; no question marks, no nuances...these are apt to confuse the visitor. (No wonder museum catalogues are hardly the stuff of academic promotion...).

e. (The National Museum) caters to a wide audience and a large one, in effect to crowds, so one must streamline one's production so that it can be swallowed "on the go." A film should not last more than six minutes; a text should be short enough to be read practically while walking. The public does not want to be taught; so one has to be catchy, emphasize the spectacular....

f. Above all, we do not want trouble. Any error means trouble. Check and recheck your text...to make sure nobody may be offended—or—Heaven forbid—disagree with anything shown or said there....

g. And finally:

— No personal statement, please
— Be optimistic
— But be serious — this is the people's TAX money, remember.

I quoted Dr. Guedon at length because she identifies with precision and eloquence three issues I want to consider: the ways in which administrative and public duties interfere with personal research, why individual interests are subordinated to collective and hierarchical responsibilities, and how the educational intent of anthropology exhibits is inhibited by the requirement to reduce all text to a lowest common denominator (no error, no offence, no personal opinion, and no big words).

The third point, how simplification may dilute the educational mission of the museum, I discuss elsewhere (Chapter 7, "Are museums and anthropology really necessary anymore?"). The point I make there is that the error lies not in the requirement to simplify, but in the expectation that anthropology exhibits are educational in the sense that they can effectively convey cognitive information. I suggest that, to the contrary, museum exhibits are relatively ineffective instruments for conveying knowledge, at least as they are typically constituted in museums today. No wonder Dr. Guedon experienced frustration in her exhibit work; there was no way she could succeed. I would like to reserve further discussion of this point for another time, however.

Here I want to consider the other two problems Dr. Guédon highlighted: the conflict between research and other museum duties, and between individual and collective interests. These conflicts have been features of museum work, on an increasing scale, ever since museums accepted the mandate to increase their services to the public. When in 1914 Edward Sapir was thinking of moving from the National Museum in Canada to a United States museum, Franz Boas advised him as follows (quoted in Darnell 1976: 117 and Halpin 1983: 262):

> The fundamental difficulty that you would find everywhere is that all purely scientific work, particularly the work in which you are interested, would have to be done as a side issue, and that the essential interest of the museum is not exploration, but the exhibit, and ordinarily the popular exhibit...I understand from your previous remarks that the administrative work that you have to do in Canada worries you and is not particularly sympathetic to you; but please do not believe that in any position that you may take, you will be relieved of this kind of work in one form or another, least of all in a museum position.

How can museums and those working within them resolve these conflicts, the "curator's dilemma"? One way, and the approach favoured by many large civic and district museums, is to abandon all pretence at research except that which is directly related to exhibit and collection needs. In some of these museums, in fact, the curatorial contract explicitly excludes personal research from the list of official duties. Curators in such institutions become "librarians" to their collections and information officers to the public, expected to know a little about everything the museum holds, but not too much about any one thing.

A second solution, and the one most commonly attempted by major museums, is to increase the opportunities, facilities and rewards for research (Sturtevant 1969: 636). This is usually attempted in the form of a binary organizational structure, with one section, higher in prestige, for the "scientists" who are expected to conduct important research, and a second section for "museologists," "administrators," and "educators," who are expected to manage the collections and public programmes. Only the very large museums with multi-million dollar annual operating budgets can afford to maintain this kind of differentiated structure. The differentiation is frequently expressed in architecture as well as in social organization. Canada's National Museum of Man, for example, has its public galleries in downtown Ottawa, while its store rooms and "scientific" staff are hidden away in the suburbs. (There are plans for a new facility which would consolidate much of what is now physically separated.) The Provincial Museum of British Columbia has a large squat building devoted to exhibits, which is open free to the public seven days a week. The reserve collections and the curators, on the other hand, reside in a carefully guarded tower nearby and access to it can only be obtained by appointment. The British Museum of Mankind in London has its public galleries in the centre of the city, only a few minutes walk from Piccadilly, and its reserve collections miles away in an old warehouse. Where the curators are, I have no idea. Though one is sometimes able to get them on the telephone, one does not often have the chance to actually meet them in person. Assistants working in the "Students' Room" adjacent to the public galleries at the Museum of Mankind are apparently responsible for screening visitors, and they do a marvelous job of politely discouraging inquiries.

The benefits of a binary organizational division between private scholarship and public service are obvious: the scientists would be given time to pursue their personal research interests while more practical people are charged with the day-to-day responsibilities of running the museum, and since they are typically lower in rank and academic training, they are not expected to have scholarly aspirations nor, thus, scholarly frustrations. It is as if every museum should be a Smithsonian with a few Barnums on staff to entertain the public, thus allowing scientists to do the real work behind the scenes. This arrangement does not always work, however. Scientists are frequently drawn into the daily museum enterprise because of its collaborative nature, as Dr. Guedon's lament documents, and many of the curatorial assistants cannot ignore their own intellectual aspirations or the higher status and rates of pay that research roles provide.

Dr. Guedon hoped that by moving to a university department she could escape burdensome administrative and public duties, and perhaps she can. Museum scientists who close their office doors, as she put it, may also be able to avoid many irksome tasks. But what kind of solution is this? One of the problems the profession of ethnology faces today—and at least in Canada it is said to be a crisis of major proportions (Tremblay 1983)—lies precisely in this scholarly withdrawal from responsibilities to the broader community of students, colleagues, and the general public. Have ethnologists, as part of their collective scorn for the crass showmanship of Barnum and his industrious fleas, or Disney and his mice and ducks, derogated as well the whole idea of private scholars performing public service? In rejecting Barnum and Disneyland we may have rejected too much.

It is understandable that academics trained in the university tradition of competitive individual scholarship would find little merit or personal reward in teamwork organized to serve broader interests. But here again lies a source of difficulty for the profession of ethnology. Traditional notions of scholarly autonomy are being called into question as our societies become more democratic. It no longer seems to be sufficient to say that scholarly work is justified provided it serves the interest of "theory" or "the progress of sciences"; it now must *also* serve broader public interests.

The eminent Canadian ethnologist Marc-Adélard Tremblay said recently (1983: 332) that anthropology is undergoing a serious crisis that is threatening the very foundations of the discipline. Its traditional objectives, methodologies and findings are all being called into question We must analyze our weaknesses, he said, and consider alternative courses of action so that we might, in the end, "come up with ideas and suggestions instrumental in redefining our objectives, in discovering new paths for gaining knowledge and in sharpening our guidelines for the practising of anthropology" (1983: 341).

Attempts to resolve professional role conflicts brought about by the progress of democracy by, for example, separating research scholars from applied workers, or by seeking the seclusion of an ivory tower, only succeed in postponing the resolution. It may be more productive to directly confront the conflicts and tensions, and to admit the possibility that we may have to change the way in which we conduct our work.

Museums have been subjected to the pressures of democratization more than have universities because they have been more closely integrated into the daily life of their communities and therefore more fully appropriated by those communities. Perhaps, therefore, we should look to museums for hints as to how our profession may evolve over the next several decades. Anthropology museums, which purport to be the storehouses of the past, may also be windows onto the future.

I conclude by citing the conclusion to a paper written by a colleague of mine at the University of British Columbia Museum of Anthropology, Dr. Marjorie Halpin, who serves both as a curator of ethnology in the museum and as an associate professor of anthropology in the university's Department of Anthropology. The title of her paper, which she delivered to a conference convened in 1981 to assess the state of Canadian ethnology, is "Anthropology as Artefact." This title, she says (Halpin 1983: 273):

> is meant to suggest that the situation of the ethnologist in museums is not unique, but that the bureaucratic museum context permits us to see more clearly than the university context the choices facing all scholars as we approach the 21st century. When we become clear as to what our choices are, it becomes ever clearer that we have no choice. We can either (1) recognize the conflicts, contradictions, and pretences that reside in the condition of museum ethnology, and ride those contradictions, as creative opportunities, or (2) recognize the condition and despair. At the Museum of Anthropology, we have resolved to ride the contradictions in search of a new mandate as ethnologists. We invite our academic colleagues to examine the museum for a glimpse into a possible future.

The solution, it would appear, lies neither in becoming showmen like Barnum nor in retreating behind the closed doors of secluded offices, but in charting a path somewhere between, where the dignity of serious scholarship combines with the nobility of public service.

NOTES

1. I would like to thank Margaret Meikle, University of British Columbia Museum of Anthropology, for information that assisted in the preparation of this chapter.

2. Evel Knievel is an American daredevil who earned several million dollars during the 1970's riding his motorcycle over buses and canyons.

3

What Could a Social Anthropologist Do in a Museum of Anthropology?[1]

The Anthropology of Museums and Anthropology

A few years ago Professor Robin Ridington, a colleague of mine in the University of British Columbia Department of Anthropology, wrote a paper entitled, "What is a Clown Doing in the Museum of Anthropology?"[2] He was considering the role of Garbanzo, the anthropology-trained professional clown who regularly performs at the university's Museum of Anthropology, where I also work, and at anthropological conferences in North America (Gibbons 1983).

Ridington concluded that it was appropriate to locate a clown in a museum because he is an effective teacher, bringing the collections alive through mime and story-telling. "The clown's introduction to the artefacts and images in the Museum of Anthropology," Ridington wrote (1979: 90), "is true to the spirit of native teaching in that it creates a situation in which, without words, knowledge of the transformative vision is strengthened." The clown-teacher shows children how to see as well as what to see. He takes children, and adults, through a looking-glass land into the world of images and ideas.

What is interesting about Professor Ridington's argument, and also Garbanzo's performance, is how readily other anthropologists are willing to agree that it is a great idea. Anthropologists do not seem to have any problem understanding what a clown might be doing in an anthropology museum.

When one asks the question, "what might a social anthropologist[3] be doing in a museum of anthropology?", on the other hand, members of the anthropological profession appear less certain of the answer. Clowns belong in museums all right, but do social anthropologists? Judging by the attitudes expressed by many of our colleagues, social anthropologists belong in museums if they take to clowning, as anthropologist Paul Gibbons has done in the form of Garbanzo, or perhaps if they are seeking to retire from the rigors of academic life; but it is difficult to think of any other sensible reason for them to be there. In fact, during this century there has been a steady shift by anthropologists from museums towards universities and colleges, and as the location where most anthropologists work has changed, so also has the nature of their work.

During the early history of anthropology it was closely tied to museums, which provided the principal institutional bases and financial support for research. Sturtevant (1969:662) refers to this beginning phase as the "Museum Period," running from about 1840 to 1890, at least in North America. By the 1880's universities in United States and England began to offer training in anthropology, taught for the first while mostly by anthropologists who also held museum positions. Sturtevant names this the "Museum-University Period," running up to the 1920s. (He notes that similar developments occurred in Europe and elsewhere, though perhaps beginning earlier at least in Europe, so his chronology should be adjusted accordingly when applied outside North America.)

The "University Period" of anthropology began in North America in the 1920's, and within ten to twenty years the majority of anthropologists had moved full time into teaching institutions, and universities and foundations had taken over support of most field work (Sturtevant 1969: 624). Where anthropologists were once closely associated in museums with zoologists, botanists, and other natural scientists interested in the study of concrete materials, as they moved into academic environments they began to associate more closely with social and behavioural scientists who were more concerned with symbolic or ideational components of culture. University-based anthropology became more social science oriented in methodology and more "mentalist" in its interests, increasingly interested in studying the mental or ideational products of primitive man—or, at least, the products as reconstructed by anthropologists—rather than studying what primitive people did and made. Early manifestations of this approach, which Harris (1979) characterizes as "cultural idealism," went under the rubrics of structural functionalism, culture and personality, cognitive anthropology, and structuralism. Terms heard today include psychological anthropology, symbolic anthropology, semiotics, and hermeneutics.

Anthropological interest in the study of material culture and in museums steadily declined as anthropologists themselves moved away from the museum environment. In their 1954 review of the role of the museums in anthropology, Collier and Tschopik asked whether the study of material culture had by then become a "dead duck," and they concluded that essentially it had. And this "alienation" of anthropology from museums is continuing, Maurice Freedman (1979:54) observed in his 1979 *Main Trends in Social and Cultural Anthropology.* If anything, the poor old material culture duck is more dead than ever.

Museum anthropologists frequently express embarrassment and dismay over the lack of attention they receive from their colleagues. "Anthropology is in the situation," Sturtevant remarked (1969: 625), "of having the responsibility for huge and irreplaceable collections which represent a large investment over many years of time, thought, and money, but seemingly have very little importance for current anthropological research, especially ethnological research." Sturtevant estimates there are some four and one-half million ethnological artefacts stored in museums around the world (1969: 640), most only a few hundred years old, and perhaps as much as 90 per cent never studied (1969: 632).

There are various reasons why museum collections attract little scholarly attention. In the first place, many items are not worth studying anyway, either because they are intrinsically uninteresting or because they lack sufficient data concerning provenance, function, or meaning. Second, many museums, ironically, offer meager facilities to researchers and some seem inclined to discourage visiting scholars. Museum storerooms, especially those associated with large museums, are difficult to gain access to, and museum staff are usually too busy with other matters to provide much assistance. A third reason is the absence of important theoretical issues in material culture studies. Research on museum collections actually never did play an important role in the development of ethnological theories (Sturtevant 1969: 621-23,632), though it did in archaeology and it was more relevant to ethnology earlier than now, and though museums provided employment for many ethnologists. And there has been little theoretical development associated with material culture research itself. General questions are seldom being asked or answered, and ideas derived from collections research are rarely being related to broader intellectual or professional issues in anthropology, with the exceptions of art and archaeology. Museum ethnologists need to do more theoretical work, to develop both theories of the object and theories of the museum.

The prevailing attitude today in anthropology towards museum anthropology, to summarize my first point, is that it is drifting about in the swampy backwaters of the discipline, suitable only for clowns and dead ducks. This attitude is generated in part by the academic setting to which most anthropologists have shifted in order to do their work. Today, in fact, most anthropologists know very little about museums. As Nancy Oestreich Lurie, Curator of Anthropology at the Milwaukee Public Museum, noted in a 1981 paper (1981: 181), "Whole generations of anthropologists have now completed professional careers without ever having had to set foot in a museum...." At the 1979 Canadian Ethnology Society meetings, to give another example, museums were included in a list of *new* areas of prospective employment for young anthropologists.

My next point concerns how the conditions of work that prevail in museums today differ from those found in universities, and the influence these differences have on the kind of anthropological work that gets done and could be done.

Museums have not remained static since anthropologists began fleeing from them 40 to 50 years ago. In contrast to universities, which have maintained a degree of autonomy and insulation from the communities that support them, museums for better or for worse have become more closely integrated into and involved with the communities in which they are located, and thus, in a sense, more "democratized" than universities. Museum personnel, therefore, necessarily have had to become more responsive to a wider public, including especially to those they study and from whom they collect, from whom they draw their visitors, and from whom they obtain funding for museum operations. Academic anthropologists, on the other hand, are still, by and large, responsible only to their professional peers and to foundations that provide personal research grants. They do not have to answer, except in a more generalized way, to the public, to the Board of Trustees, or even to the people they study.

Ethnology, by the nature of its style of research—the solitary investigator spending a year or more "in the field" as a participant-observer—has few reality-testing mechanisms. Anthropologists rarely check the work of their colleagues through systematic replication, being content instead with comparing a personal interpretation of one's "own" village or tribe or clutch of informants with the interpretations advanced by other anthropologists on the bases of their personal field experiences. Much depends upon how cleverly one can argue the case for or against some idea.

Museum anthropologists share these personalized reality-testing mechanisms that are internal to our discipline; but their work is subjected to external testing as well because of the higher visibility and interdisciplinary nature of the work they do. The products of their endeavours will be reviewed by other professionals in the museum community, by the governing bodies, by the general public, and, perhaps most important of all, by members of the populations they study and exhibit. University anthropologists usually do not have to deal with the people they study except on their own terms, such as when they go into the field and treat people as informants or when they recruit them as students. In both instances the academic anthropologist determines the occasion for interaction and places the "native" in a subordinate role. These same natives are likely to march into a museum any day of the week, on the other hand, and expect — quite rightly — to be treated with the same respect that other visitors receive. Also, because museums are highly visible public institutions associated with the establishment, they and their representatives are particularly vulnerable to public criticism. Scholars working within universities are more insulated from any negative consequences of such criticism.

There are other ways in which the conditions of work for museum anthropologists differ from those for university counterparts. Most museum work is practical or applied rather than "pure," and collaborative rather than solitary. Curators must work closely with technicians, designers, conservators, educators, business administrators and volunteers in a process of cooperative production. Academics also engage in group work, for example co-teaching, co-editing, and joint research, but occasionally rather than routinely, and they collaborate less frequently with such a broad range of specialists or across the boundaries of the pure and the applied.

We need to consider one important structural difference within the museum community, between curatorial roles in museums of history and anthropology, on the one hand, and the counterpart roles in galleries and museums of art, on the other. The differences are particularly clear in approaches to exhibitions and other public programming, and they help to explain the lower esteem in which anthropology and history curating is sometimes held.[4]

Curators of history and anthropology are concerned with the reconstruction of what they judge to be the original contexts of their specimens, to display them in a fabricated originality, as it were. This requires considerable cleverness and technical skill, but not much original scholarship. Research is directed mostly towards identifying the provenance and function of particular objects and then translating this information into palatable educational packages for the public (Guédon 1983). Curating an anthropology or history exhibit is like writing an elementary textbook with a liberal use of visual aids. The exhibit is based on scholarly work usually already published, and it certainly consumes a major part of the curator's time; but it is not itself, in the typical case, considered to be original scholarly research.

Curators in galleries and museums of art, on the other hand, and the art community to which they are connected, regard an art exhibit as an "original scholarly statement" in its own right. This is because the selection and presentation of works of art are expected to be an informed personal interpretation by a knowledgeable person, an "expert" Art exhibits are regarded as (National Museums of Canada 1982: 2),

> a means of contributing to a dialogue within the artistic community regarding artists, their work, their significance, their acceptance over time, and their influence upon each other. These latter considerations are largely irrelevant to the objectives of museums and their exhibition policies...which (are) directed almost solely at (the) public.

To summarize my second point: the social organization of museum work makes museum anthropologists more visible, and therefore more vulnerable, than their university counterparts. Much of their work is interdisciplinary and collaborative, and concerned more with interpretation than with original discovery. This is a situation that produces excitement or despair according to the nature of the individual. Some of those working in museums try to close their office doors and concentrate on their own personal work to the exclusion of other responsibilities, a regular practice in Academe but rarely possible in museums except perhaps the large and wealthy ones. Other museum anthropologists submerge themselves in the practical day-to-day work of collections management and public education, engaging in research only for the purposes of artefact identification and text book exhibitions, thus, in effect, renouncing their scholarly aspirations.

Neither alternative seems very attractive, either to hide from the world or to submerge oneself in busy work; nor am I myself qualified — the criticism of some of my colleagues notwithstanding — to serve as a museum clown. So I return to my first question: What can a social anthropologist do in a museum of anthropology? Given the conditions of work and the opportunities and constraints they entail, what can one do that is worth doing? This leads me to the third point I want to make: because of the peculiar structural position of museums in modern society they provide a fertile ground for pure and applied research on a variety of topics and for the development of anthropological theory relevant to our present concerns.

I will give an example of what I mean. Several years ago I visited one of our former students who was at that time managing a small museum in a town about 800 miles north of Vancouver (Canada). She showed me around the museum and talked about the town and her position in it. As the curator-director of the museum, she had to deal with a number of people, to seek support for her institution, and to promote better understanding of the heritage of both the native Indians and European settlers. Part way through our conversation she stopped and said to me, apologetically, "but I never get time to do any research here!" Trained as an anthropologist in the university mold, research meant to her the study of native Indians and their ancestral traditions. She did not realize the amount of informal research on local politics she had carried out in order to do her job. She had sketched for me during our conversation a sociological portrait, in rich detail, of who governs and who matters in this small town. That was great stuff, but she did not think of it as research or as something she might one day want to write about.

We now train our students to be more reflexive, to critically inspect and write about their own work situations and to do the ethnography of their own museums. We could call this "practising anthropology in our own backyards" (Ames 1979).

I mentioned earlier how most museum research focuses on objects in the attempt to retrieve information about them, to subject them to stylistic analyses, or to prepare them for public exhibition. There are other ways of looking at objects, however, that will open up many more possibilities for social anthropological research. One way is to extend the idea of the object to include the museum itself, as an artefact of our own society; and another way is to examine the social history of the objects, especially in their reconstructed contexts.

The study of the organization of museums and their role in the community are ways of viewing museums as artefacts. Small museums, for example, provide opportunities to explore such topics as the interpersonal dynamics within small groups, the role differentiation between professional and amateur anthropologists and historians (Cannizzo 1979; Vallance 1981), and the genesis of a community's collective representations (Cannizzo 1982; Halpin 1983; Singer 1977).

I have myself investigated ways in which anthropologists and museums contribute to the redefinition of the peoples they study, helping to manufacture their own objects of research (Ames 1981b). (I will have more to say about this in chapter 5, "How anthropologists create the cultures they study".)

Another way to view museums as objects is to view their activities and programmes as cultural performances, an approach derived from the work of Milton Singer (1972). That is to say, an exhibition in which a museum presents the artefacts of another culture may itself be examined as an artefact of our own. We look for the unintended messages conveyed along with the official ones. The best example of this approach I know about is provided by one of our own curators at the University of British Columbia Museum of Anthropology, Dr. Marjorie Halpin (1978). She reviewed a new anthropological gallery at a nearby museum, and in the course of her review outlined her approach. An exhibit, she says, should be seen as a cultural performance or statement made not only about native cultures but also about ourselves. Looked at in this way, "We can perhaps see how much more we are saying than intended."

I quote from her article, published in the Journal of the Canadian Museums Association in 1978 (p. 41):

> This is rather a delicate approach, for we swim so securely in the waters of our own culture that it is hard to see. Even sophisticated anthropologists seem at times to operate in terms of an implicit assumption that the rest of the world's peoples swim unknowingly in culture, whereas we deal directly and rationally with reality. What we need is a mechanism for estranging ourselves from ourselves in order to see ourselves, to pierce the veil of comfort and necessity within which cultural activities perforce seem right and proper. We need to become the anthropologists of ourselves. But perhaps that is too grandiose. We can, however, learn to see something of how we reflect ourselves in the exhibits we invent about others, just as we can find ourselves reflected in cereal boxes, automobiles, leisure suits, billboards, television, and textbooks.

The exhibition Dr. Halpin reviewed deals with the history and culture of the Indians of British Columbia, the westernmost province of Canada. It combines a superb collection of Northwest Coast artefacts all packaged in a superly constructed exhibition involving advanced exhibition design and technology. The exhibition demonstrates the past artistic achievements of local Indians combined with a more subtle message about the present technological sophistication of the museum's designers, technicians and curators. As Halpin observed (1978: 47)

> ...to walk through these galleries, contrasting the Indian cultural performance with our own, is to learn as much about ourselves as them. Even more, it is to *see* the clash of two cultures and *experience* the technological and political ascendancy of one at the expense of the other. (Emphasis in the original.)

Museums also provide convenient locations for practising ethnographic techniques that can be used in programme evaluation and impact assessment studies. The ethnographic method is increasingly being utilized in evaluation work (Alexander 1981; Britan 1978a, 1978b; Wolf 1980), so it makes sense to give our students some practical training along these lines (Ames 1979). What better place for a practicum is there than a museum with exhibits and other public and educational programmes, the description and assessment of which would benefit both the museum and the student?

For those anthropologists who prefer to focus on material objects, rather than on social objects like museums, there are still ways to broaden the research agenda. The traditional purpose for studying objects, as I mentioned above, is to identify or reconstruct their original, or at least earlier, settings, with a focus upon the properties, provenance, use, and meaning of those objects. The possibilities for useful theoretical results are limited, however, because there is seldom sufficient information about the original or earlier contexts of museum collections to pursue questions very far. This may change somewhat as we are able to mak more extensive use of sophisticated analytical techniques, but the fact remains that traditional material culture research so far has not answered many theoretically important questions.

There is another area of research, still centering on the object, for which data can be gathered, however, concerning what might be called the "recontextualization of the object" (Halpin 1983). By that I mean the social history of the object: the study of what happens to objects, and to the people they attract, once they leave the hands of the original users, and most particularly, once they become appropriated by scholars, collectors, and museums in the wealthier nations. Objects live beyond their origins, and acquire new meanings, new uses, and new owners along the way. As Stephen Inglis, one of our students who has done material culture research both in India and Canada, noted in a recent paper on Canadian folk art (1982), there is a patina that develops on the surface of the study of objects as well as on the surface of the objects themselves, and the study of this conceptual patina will reveal to us currents in intellectual history. In his 1978 review of anthropology, Maurice Freedman said that the museum was a "palace of the concrete and...a machine for decontextualization". He was only partly right. Museums — and also scholars, collectors, and others — certainly remove objects from their earlier contexts (and not always with full respect for local laws and customs, one might add); but through this process of removal they place those objects into new contexts, the contexts of our own history and culture. And this process of *recontextualization* or redefinition should be of interest to anthropology, for it not only informs us about ourselves but also about recurring features of culture contact, culture domination, and culture change.

The study of the arts of acculturation and the transformation of tribal arts from archaic specimens to tourist souvenirs to fine art (Graburn 1976) is a good example of what I mean by the study of the process of reconstruction of the object or of its social history. These studies would increase our understanding of the processes of social change and how they affect populations at risk, and they might also assist those populations in coping with change (Appell 1977: 15; 1980). Karen Duffek, another one of our students—to give another example—examined the production and marketing of native Indian handicrafts in British Columbia and was able to identify effects the market had on style, quality, and quantity of objects produced by indigenous craftsmen. Her work illustrates how multi-faceted museum research can become when it is conducted in a reflexive manner with an eye towards practical as well as theoretical applications. In the course of her research, Duffek mounted a small exhibit of contemporary Indian crafts in the University Museum of Anthropology and interviewed museum visitors to find out the criteria they used to judge native works. In addition to completing her thesis (1983c), she produced a consumer guide for the general public (1983a), presented and published scholarly papers (1983b, 1983d and 1985), and contributed to the revision of the Museum of Anthropology's policies on the acquisition, exhibition and sale of contemporary Indian art.

I began this chapter by considering whether social anthropologists have useful roles to play in museums, besides, that is, those of textbook writers or clown-teachers. After commenting on the distancing relations between academic anthropology and museums and their different structural settings, I reviewed some of the research activities in which social anthropologists in and around museums are presently engaged. My examples were mostly limited to the Museum of Anthropology, though other examples could be cited. As Butler and Horn noted in a recent issue of the United States journal *Museum News* (1983: 43), "Recent efforts include research in education, the analysis of visitor behaviour and philanthropic behaviour in a community, museum management practices, marketing, communications systems and the sociology of museums."

I will now summarize by presenting two general conclusions regarding museums and their relevance for social anthropology.

First, museums are representations of the societies in which they are situated (MacCannell 1976). They are repositories of culture, machines for recontextualization, and platforms for the creation and promotion of cultural heritage. As such, they provide numerous opportunities for social anthropologists to examine cultural patterns and cultural properties as they are actually being conceived, practised, manufactured, transformed, disseminated, used, and misused. By studying museums in their social and historical settings we can study the making of culture in its concrete reality.

Second, museums are also scholarly institutions with unique benefits and defects (McFeat 1962). They are repositories of data; they encourage long term research; they facilitate joint and shared work; they disseminate knowledge to wider publics; and they are obliged to relate directly with publics beyond specialized disciplines. This public dimension of museum life constitutes a great stress for some members of these institutions and a powerful stimulus for others; but either way the situation provides opportunities for individuals to hone their traditional anthropological skills and to acquire new ones, and to use their anthropological knowledge in their daily work as well as in their occasional research. The challenging environment of modern museums provides opportunities for creative innovations in the theories and methods of anthropology.

NOTES

1. An earlier version of this chapter was presented in a paper to the Annual Meeting of the Canadian Ethnology Society, Vancouver, Canada, May 11, 1982.

2. Unfortunately for the title of my paper, Ridington changed the title of his to "Mirrors and Masks" when he published it (1979).

3. I use the terms social anthropology and ethnology interchangeably to refer to the sociocultural branch of anthropology, which is customarily distinguished from archaeology, physical anthropology and linguistics. Ethnology is frequently used in the museum context and social anthropology almost never.

4. In making this distinction I draw heavily upon an unpublished note prepared in 1982 by the Museums Assistance Programme of the National Museums of Canada, entitled "Exhibition Assistance Programme and Museums of Human and Natural History, Science and Technology."

4

How Anthropologists Stereotype Other People[1]

I want to consider the ways in which anthropology, particularly through its museums, structures the ways we think about other cultures. As one of the social sciences, anthropology attempts to produce "objective knowledge" about the world, particularly the world of other cultures. Presumably these objective productions are represented in the exhibitions presented by anthropology museums. When we examine the history of museum exhibitry, however, we discover changes in philosophy and style. What museums once thought was the objective truth subsequently becomes no longer fashionable. Museum exhibitions thus appear to reflect, or to exhibit, the changing images of other cultures that anthropologists have produced during the course of their work. Even though anthropologists may be engaged in scientific research, they nevertheless also actively help to construct the phenomena they study

I will describe four ways ethnographic collections have been displayed in museums, from the early Curiosity Cabinets to the most modern exhibitions in major American museums, to illustrate how each approach, both subtly and explicitly, characterizes in a particular manner the arts and crafts of third world peoples and ethnic minorities, the traditional subjects of anthropology museums. Each of these exhibit philosophies is derived from a different set of assumptions about what constitutes the proper study of the works of humankind, and each has played an important role in determining how museums present anthropological information through museum exhibitions. These four perspectives may be represented by different museums, by stages in the evolution of a particular museum, or by the separate components of a single large museum. The great Smithsonian Institution in the United States, for example, developed many exhibition styles over the years and at least one for each of its divisional museums. As Lowless and Cohen describe the situation in their article on the "Smithsonian Style" (1977: 59):

> Each (Smithsonian) museum approached its collection in its own way — in the museums of art with a taste for beauty and simplicity, in the history museums with a passion for the excesses and variety that is the story of the American genius, in the science exhibits with explicit demonstrations of the structural facets of our technological civilization.

As important as these approaches are, however, they all are rejected by proponents of another perspective I will describe, which has emerged in recent years and is strongly critical of the very idea of anthropology museums.

1. Cabinets of Curiosities

The first perspective I want to discuss is usually associated with the foundation of museums and therefore actually precedes the development of professional anthropological perspectives.

Several hundred years ago and more the material properties of tribal peoples were classed with strange flora and fauna, as objects of wonder and delight, to be collected as trophies, souvenirs, or amusing curiosities during one's travels to far and distant lands.

Cabinets featuring collections of both natural and artificial exotica became a common feature of royal and noble households throughout Europe during the sixteenth and seventeenth centuries, forming "Cabinets of Curiosities," "Cabinets of Rarities," or "Houses of Curios," as they came to be called (MacGregor 1983).

These cabinets were unsystematic and idiosyncratic in composition, and were filled to the point of overflowing. It was common practice for travellers to bring back whatever they could find that was strange or wonderful, as illustrations of their adventures in newly contacted or recently colonized lands abroad. What was important was to select objects that would stimulate admiration and wonder and which would reflect upon the daring exploits, special knowledge, or privileged status of the collector. These cabinets of curiosities provided the foundations for major museum collections in Europe, and the curiosity they provoked contributed to the development of a scientific interest in the study of cultural and natural materials.

The major museums of the world have long since replaced the idea of curiosity cabinets, however, through their introduction of systematic collecting, analytical classifications, and educational displays. There has been considerable progress and increasing sophistication during the past hundred years in the management and exhibition of museum collections, as museum workers themselves become more professionalized leading to the development of new ways of presenting the object.

2. Early Anthropology Museums and the Natural History Approach

"Cabinets of Curiosities" were gradually transformed into organized museums as museum staff professionalized themselves and their conditions of work (Baxi 1973: 60; Frese 1960:8). By the latter part of the nineteenth century, while anthropology was emerging as a distinctive discipline in the universities, anthropological museums began to take shape as well. Both the profession of anthropology and anthropological museums were outgrowths of the nineteenth century expansion of western imperialism and rationalism (Frese 1960: 194). A typical objective of early anthropological displays was, therefore, to present artefacts from primitive societies as if they were specimens akin to those of natural history. Following the tradition of the Cabinets of Curiosities, primitive peoples were considered to be parts of nature like the flora and fauna, and therefore their arts and crafts were to be classified and presented according to similarity of form, evolutionary stage of development, or geographical origin. The comparative theme was the essential ingredient. (For examples, see Thomas Wilson's 1891 report of anthropology exhibits at the 1889 Paris exposition and Burton Benedict's 1983 *The Anthropology of World's Fairs,* especially pp. 45-52.) This early anthropological perspective can still be found in many museums of natural and human history around the world. The great Pitt Rivers Museum at the University of Oxford is perhaps the best example (Blackwood 1970).

3. Modern Anthropology and Contextualism

The modern anthropological approach to museums developed out of this background associated with natural history, and, at least in North America, it owes much to a German immigrant and founder of professional anthropology in the New World, Franz Boas.

Boas's first serious involvement with museum work was when he supervised the arrangement of ethnological collections for the Chicago Exposition in 1893, collections which subsequently formed the nucleus of the Chicago Field Museum. He next went to the American Museum of Natural History in New York where he installed native Indian displays in the galleries there. Through these installations Boas popularized a different form of anthropological display, exhibiting artefacts in fabricated settings that simulated the original cultural contexts from which they came, rather than as natural history specimens representing some typology or evolutionary sequence. Artefacts should be grouped together to illustrate a way of life, he said, and that way of life—the context—would give the artefacts their meaning (Mead and Bunzel 1960: 305; Stocking 1971: 155-156).

The idea of artificially contextualizing through the craft of an exhibit designer the data or specimens from other cultures is justified by the assumption that this is necessary if we are to see objects from the "native point of view"; that is, how they were used in their original context. According to Boas and his followers, it is the mission (though a self-appointed one) of anthropology to present the native point of view, and creating contextualized exhibits is the normal way anthropology museums attempt to fulfil that mission. On a more general level, contextual exhibits are designed to answer two questions (Adams 1981: 292, 296): How can collections add to the understanding of other societies? and how can collections be used to illuminate anthropological concepts and insights? Some anthropologists mistakenly believe that these two questions are identical.

4. The Formalist Perspective: Ethnographic Specimens as Fine Art

Looking at objects as curiosities was the first perspective I described. Treating them as specimens of natural history was the second perspective, an early version of anthropological exhibiting. Presenting objects as representatives of a cultural context—the objects becoming words and sentences in a three-dimensional story about a people and their lifeways—is the third perspective and is the point of view that today finds the widest appeal in anthropology museums (Frese 1960: 51, 104, 211).

A fourth way of looking at objects is also attributed to Boas's inspiration, though ironically it seriously challenges the contextualist view he promoted and takes us back closer to the principle of curiosity. This fourth point of view, which we may call the aesthetic or formalist perspective, looks at the material culture of primitive societies for examples of the fine art; form becomes more important than content.

When the Metropolitan Museum of Art in New York City opened its Michael Rockefeller Wing of primitive art several years ago it proudly proclaimed that primitive art finally has been recognized and has taken "an equal footing" with the great art of the world. "Today," wrote Douglas Newton (1981: 10), the Chairman of the Met's Department of Primitive Art, in the catalogue issued in conjunction with the opening of this gallery, "attention is paid to the work of art from another tradition for its own sake, its own identity, even when it comes from so remote a source as one of the world's primitive cultures." (New York always likes to believe it is first, but similar statements were made years earlier by other museums, including, for example, the National Museum of Man in Ottawa, the Provincial Museum in British Columbia, the Museum of Anthropology at the University of British Columbia, and so on. A number of museums in Europe could be cited as well.)

It was Boas, Newton stated in the catalogue (ibid., p. 9), who evoked the word "beauty," so rarely used before in the analysis of tribal materials, and it was he who insisted on the existence of aesthetic knowledge among all peoples, and therefore, presumably, our right to view the creations of primitive people as aesthetic objects and to subject those works to formal analysis.

Some formalists reject the contextualist approach on the grounds that it is no less an arbitrary arrangement than the old curiosity cabinet, because the simulated context of the exhibition represents the mental reconstruction of the anthropologist further elaborated by the technical artistry of the exhibit designer. Such exhibitions, the formalists suggest, may tell us as much about our own exhibit technology and fashionable theories as they do about the cultures contextualized therein.

The contextualists, on the other hand, reject the formalist perspective as being completely inappropriate for a museum of anthropology. Taking specimens "out of context"—that is, displaying them as art objects—is considered immoral by many anthropologists. An eminent British anthropologist, for example, recently dismissed all museums with the damning phrase that they were merely "machines for de-contextualization" (Freedman 1978: 54).

Though the formalists and contextualists hold opposing doctrines, they are usually willing to tolerate differences providing the formalists remain in art museums and the contextualists remain in their museums of anthropology and natural history. Only when boundaries are crossed do people get agitated or confused. If a museum of anthropology displays the material workings of a tribal society as fine art, on the other hand, then a boundary is violated, categories have become mixed, and people are likely to become disoriented and upset.

I will summarize the perspectives so far considered. I described four different ways museums look at, think about, and present strange objects, and thus attempt as well to structure the way we look at and think about those objects. Museums may present objects as curiosities, as natural history specimens, as contextual elements, or as fine art. Though there are important differences between these approaches, and some are today more popular than others, they nevertheless share in common certain features that set them apart from a fifth perspective that is to be considered.

First, all four approaches are comparative in outlook. They attempt to place particular objects into wider contexts of intellectual discourse and analysis. However much distortion this process of comparison involves, it is also a necessary aid to generalization.

Second, all four are imperfect. Though each may be fashionable in certain theoretical circles, each represents only a selection of a larger totality. Each is, therefore, chronically incomplete, and even in combination they do not represent the whole.

The third characteristic these four perspectives share is the fact that they are all outsider views looking in at the past of another people (Merton 1972). Even contextualists who claim they represent the native point of view are still outsiders who are attempting through their reconstructions to simulate someone else's experience. "The display of people is a display of power," Burton Benedict (1983: 52) concluded after surveying the ways people were exhibited at world's fairs:

> It is a symbolic performance demonstrating power relationships, but these relationships are not necessarily real. They may be idealized from the point of view of the exhibitors. They may be highly deceptive and represent a kind of symbolic wishful thinking.

They represent the thinking of outsiders, and this brings us to the fifth perspective: the insider's point of view—the native point of view from the point of view of the native him or herself.

5. The Insider's Point of View

I will give an example of what I mean.

In October 1982 the University of British Columbia Museum of Anthropology invited the Haida Indians from the Queen Charlotte

Islands, north of Vancouver, to come down and raise a new totem pole carved by one of their own. It was an exciting event, involving several thousand people, both Indian and White, working together to physically raise the pole in a simulated traditional manner. That pole is now standing on the grounds of the museum. The museum staff were very pleased about this event because it seemed to be such a great success for everyone, both Indians and Whites. We were proud that we were able to bring the groups together in a common cause. I felt very good about it myself. Shortly afterwards, however, I was talking to an Indian artist who was not involved in the pole raising but knew about it, and he brought me back down to earth very quickly.

"You know," he said to me, "you haven't done a damn thing for Indians. We don't feel at home in your museums—any of them—because they don't tell us *our* story."

> When you talk about origins you refer to archaeology and the Bering Straits, and "origin myths", "legends", and "prehistory". We don't know anything about the Bering Straits or about myths and legends. We *know* who we are and where we come from. Our elders tell us that. They speak in truths, not in myths.

His people, he continued, always had their history, which anthropologists would occasionally try to record and to describe as "mythology," "legends," or "folklore." Their own history, their insider view, increasingly has had to contend with the outsider Whiteman's views propagated by missionaries, Indian agents, teachers, and anthropologists. He admitted that some Indians eventually succumbed to the outsider views and incorporated them as their own. But others are trying to preserve, to recover, and even to re-discover their own perspectives. These are more personal views of history than any portrayed by museums. The source of true knowledge is derived from the memories of the elders rather than from the so-called objective facts of the social scientists.

Indian communities in North America have become increasingly disenchanted with anthropology, in fact, and some have gone so far as to ban anthropological research. One recent case, again among the Haida of the Queen Charlotte Islands, may serve as an example. In response to their dissatisfaction with a study of their community published by an anthropologist, the Band Council of the Massett Haida passed the following resolution. dated June 7, 1983.

> THAT WHEREAS: The Haida people of Old Masset resent the intru-

sion of anthropologists, archaeologists, and other persons who spend their time studying specimens of humanity.

AND WHEREAS: The Haida people are concerned that any information that is gathered is of no benefit to the Haida people and only benefits the social scientists in their quest for recognition.

AND WHEREAS: The Haida people have a right to live out their lives in dignity and quiet enjoyment.

AND WHEREAS: Certain individuals have made a practise of infringing upon the rights and privileges of members of the Massett Band and abused privileged information that they've gathered from the elders of the Band.

THEREFORE, BE IT RESOLVED: That the Masset Band Council ban one (X Anthropologist) from the Massett Reserve # 1 and that any information concerning the Haida people of Old Massett be returned to the Massett Band Council forthwith, and that no further contact be made with any of the members of the Massett Band.

Not only North American Indians reject the legitimacy of traditional anthropological research. Note the following statements made by Papua New Guinea students, recorded for a United States public television film called "Anthropology on Trial" (Holecek 1983: 1).

Nahua Roodney: I think, in the '80s, we must stop anthropologists coming into the country. Secondly, we have our own academics, we have our own Papua New Guineans who now can become anthropologists themselves...

Student: Sometimes they tell us, "You go to the library and you look up this book, and you read this." And sometimes we ask the lecturers, "Can we do it from our own background knowledge?" And they say, "Oh no, you have to read the books in the library." And that's why we get very upset. Why should I read a book that is written by somebody from outside, when I can tell it from my own knowledge, my own society?

Indian history from the Indian point of view is the added ingredient that is needed, the fifth perspective, in order to think about Indian objects in museums. It is not a matter of either or, an insider versus an outsider monopoly on truth. Nor is it correct to believe that the reconstructed contextualist view of the modern anthropologist is an adequate portrayal of the insider view. Insiders reject that possibility out of hand. It is, rather, a question of how the insider and outsider perspectives might interact and build upon one another in the process of truth-seeking and understanding (Merton 1972: 36).

What is this insider perspective, the so-called "Indian point of view"? First, we must immediately recognize that there is no *one* insider perspective, no one orthodoxy. Views are continuing to evolve, to formulate and to re-formulate, as times change and as generations of elders come and go. There are views of the past that may be only dimly remembered; moreover, most objects in museums belong to that dimly remembered past rather than to present generations. This is not unique to the Northwest Coast of North America; what we have here is simply an example which we may consider in order to think about objects in museums and to think about how museums try to structure the way we do that thinking.

Second, we must admit that we cannot easily characterize the insider perspectives, because to do so would be to transform them into our comparative and international languages, thereby reconstructing them like our fabricated exhibitions. Perhaps it is sufficient at this point to learn to listen to them.

I will tell you about some of the things we hear around the University of British Columbia Museum of Anthropology:

1. I already mentioned the pole raising, celebrated by some Indian people and mocked by others. Some appreciate the opportunity to publicly display their heritage, while others consider heritage to be a private affair and therefore do not wish to put themselves on display.

2. Indian people are ambivalent about the relevance of museums. A representative of a tribal council that is planning a major cultural centre on Vancouver Island, for example, said to me recently that he does not like to use the word "museum" to describe what they want. The museum is a Whiteman's institution, he explained, and we don't want that sort of thing in our culture. He said they do not want to be constrained by the limitations of the category "museum". But then his tribal council hired one of Canada's top museum exhibition designers to help design their facility, virtually guaranteeing they will end up with a traditional museum display after all.

3. Several years ago the Museum of Anthropology opened a special

exhibition of traditional Salish sculpture and engraving, the first time such works had ever been exhibited in their land of origin, and the first time younger generations of Salish people had ever seen such things. We had to borrow pieces from other museums because little now remains in the Salish area. (The Salish traditionally inhabited what is now known as Greater Vancouver and the southern part of the adjacent Vancouver Island.) Salish people bussed in from all around to see the exhibition. Most enjoyed it, I suppose. But some of the elders who came said they were saddened to see all the spirits locked up in glass cases. Perhaps the objects should have been left in the foreign museums from which they came, rather than be brought back to stimulate sad memories.

4. Some Indian people, and others as well, say it was wrong to salvage the old totem poles that now stand in museums. They should have been left to decay in their deserted villages. On the other hand, other Indian people—some of whom are not themselves descendants of totem pole cultures—say that when they stand in a place like the Great Hall of the Museum of Anthropology, where the old poles are grandly displayed, they can feel the presence of the spirits and they are filled with joy, pride, and power.

5. Some say that the poles (which were originally purchased from Indian families or band councils) should be returned to the villages of origin, or to Indian museums. Other Indian people continue to ask museums to buy or to store the traditional objects they still own.

6. Museum people habitually treat their collections with a great deal of respect and care, handling the objects gently and displaying them with reverence. We should not assume by this, however, that the original users of those objects shared our attitude of sacredness. One day an Indian gentleman came up to me in the museum and pointed to several large wolf feast dishes that we were carefully displaying, protected by "Please Do Not Touch" signs, and he said to me with a smile, "Do you see those feast dishes? When we were children they used to be stored under our house, and when the river flooded we would paddle around in them as if they were canoes."

There are many voices, many stories. They do not add up to one consistent view, nor should they, because they represent different people with different interests and experiences. We nevertheless need to listen. The articulation of native points of view may serve to remind us that outsiders do not have the final word. It is the continuing interaction between these various perspectives that is important.

I do not believe that the University of British Columbia Museum of Anthropology, for example, should attempt to present the "native point of view", which it could never do properly anyway, whether by reconstructed contextualist exhibits or by other means. It is more important for a museum to concentrate on what it can do best, which is to present its own point of view as a professional institution, recognizing the limitations that implies, and to work in partnership with the museums and cultural organizations of the "native" or indigenous peoples. A museum is only one volume in an encyclopedia of culture that is always in the process of being written. No one museum can say it all, nor should it pretend that it can.

6. Looking at Objects

I have described in this chapter some of the more prominent conceptual schemes museum people use to think about objects and to give meaning to the specimens they display: objects are presented as artificial curiosities, as specimens of nature, as elements or building blocks in reconstructed contexts, as works of fine art, and as fragments of an insider's history.

The perspective one chooses is derived from broader assumptions one holds regarding the significance of the works of human kind and the nature of knowledge. Though a perspective may be presented as the "truth", its appropriateness is determined by a particular theoretical framework. It is not necessary to renounce one's own point of view or to accept the principle of relativism, however, in order to grant the possibility that the other views also make useful contributions to knowledge. It is not a question of there being an infinite number of views with which to contend, but a limited number that may, to a degree, complement one another—providing we are willing to recognize the limitations as well as the strengths of each view.

NOTES

1. Earlier versions of this chapter were presented in a paper to the Royal Society of Canada, June 1983, subsequently to be published in the Proceedings of the Society, and to the Commission on Museums of the International Union of Anthropological and Ethnological Sciences, August 1983, both in Vancouver, Canada.

5

How Anthropologists Help to Fabricate the Cultures They Study[1]

The classical portrait of an anthropologist is one of a solitary scholar travelling off to far and distant lands in search of little known societies to record them for the sake of science and humanity. It has been a noble quest that has produced some remarkable results, from which we all have benefited. There is another side to this quest, however, that I would like to consider here, and that is the extent to which anthropologists help to create through their own work the societies they purport to be discovering.

I will consider only one limited example, the study of the arts and crafts of the Indians of the Northwest Coast of North America by anthropologists associated with museums. I will suggest however, that the creative process of reconstruction we can see operating in this one example—whereby anthropologists through their curatorial and research activities are actively contributing to the development of the phenomena which they are so busily collecting and studying—is a feature common to most ethnographic reporting.

My example concerns how museum anthropologists have assisted in the creation, promotion and distribution of "acculturated artefacts" (Graburn 1968) on the Northwest Coast of North America, thus contributing to what is now being referred to as the "renaissance" of Indian art in that area. By "acculturated artefacts" I mean those produced within the context of acculturation (see especially the work of Nelson Graburn).

The problem with which I begin is a simple one. Some twenty years ago observers were recording the disappearance of Northwest Coast

Indian art. Today people talk about its "renaissance" (Vastokas 1975; Young 1980). How did this renaissance come about, and what did anthropologists have to do with it?

British Columbia artist Jack Shadbolt wrote to a Vancouver newspaper in 1954, stating that the magnificent heritage of Northwest Coast Indian art was dying to the ground and the prospect was very bleak (Shadbolt 1954). In her *Art through the Ages,* published in 1959, Helen Gardner noted that from as early as 1910, in fact, good quality Northwest Coast Indian crafts were deteriorating "beyond recall" (Gardner 1959:623).

By the mid-1970s, however, the production and distribution of contemporary Northwest Coast Indian arts and crafts had become a multimillion dollar industry. Newspapers are now referring to the "great art bonanza" of Northwest Coast Indian art (Scott 1978). Contemporary pieces have become collector's items, eagerly sought after by both museums and private collectors alike. The carvers themselves are receiving wider and wider recognition and are increasingly being referred to, or refer to themselves, as "artists" rather than as "carvers"

There are a number of factors that may account for this renaissance of Northwest Coast Indian art during the past twenty years (Vastokas 1975). First, there is in industrialized societies a growing interest in primitive art, the search for authentic experiences, and the desire for souvenirs of touristic journeys (MacCannell 1978). Second, Indian political and cultural movements have contributed to a growing awareness among Indians of their own heritage and its value. Third, the marketplace has provided increasingly attractive rewards for both quality and quantity of production of Indian souvenirs and collectibles. A fourth significant factor has been the role of anthropologists in museums, who not only have aided the revival but also have actively participated in its genesis and in governing its direction. Museums and their anthropologists entered the marketplace in full flight, buying, evaluating, and promoting contemporary Indian arts and crafts to a remarkable degree. It is this fourth factor that will be considered here.

Influence of Museum Anthropologists

Museum anthropologists influenced Indian art and craft industries on the Northwest Coast in three ways at least: through their reconstructions of the meaning of Northwest Coast art: by promoting and legitimating art and artists, as patrons to clients; and by inverting the relationship between anthropologists and Indians, so that the patrons become clients Each of these types of influence will be discussed in turn.

1. Reconstructing the meaning of Northwest Coast Indian arts and crafts

Anthropologists produced a distinctive and widely influential interpretation of the material culture collected from the Northwest Coast. This interpretation included both a *codification* of the elements or principles of Northwest Coast Indian design, and a *redefinition* of its meaning or aesthetic quality, from a "primitive" or curio art to a "fine" or "high" art comparable to the arts of western civilization.

The codification of design elements has encouraged a standardization or rationalization of design and technique. The consequences are comparable to when customary law is transformed into written law: a general stereotyping of form and content. (Another factor that has had a counter effect is the tendency among some more advanced Indian carvers to accept in part the role model of the "modern artist", who is expected to be individualistic and experimental.) Two anthropologists in particular played leading roles in this codification process: Franz Boas and Bill Holm.

Franz Boas was not the first to do anthropological investigations on the Northwest Coast, nor was he the first to show serious interest in Northwest Coast Indian design; but he produced one of the single most influential condifications of that tradition, first published in the 1897 *Bulletin of the American Museum of Natural History* and subsequently in Chapter 6 of his *Primitive Art* (1927). He provided a masterful discussion of the elements and principles of Northwest Coast Indian art, such as the oval eye form (now called ovoid), the double curve design, split U's, split representation, and dislocation of parts, along with a set of illustrations that still rank among the best in the literature.

As Helen Codere remarked in her introduction to Boas's *Kwakiutl Ethnography* (1966: XX-XXI), "even rather superficial knowledge of the elements of this art and its symbolic and operational conventions, as Boas has analysed and described them, makes it simple to specify what is wrong with anything that is not, but only purports to be, Northwest Coast art".

Codere then went on to make a prophetic statement: "There seems to be no reason why thorough mastery of the details of Boas' analysis, with a requisite technical skill in painting or carving, should not make it possible to produce authentic new Northwest Coast art." She pointed out how this would provide a generative test of the adequacy of Boas's analysis, and this is precisely what has happened.

Bill Holm, of the University of Washington and Thomas Burke Museum, is today recognized as the leading analyst of Northwest Coast design. He took the process of codification even further than Boas, at least for two-dimensional or flat design, and produced what has become the standard text studied by both anthropologists and Indian carvers alike (Holm 1965). Holm taught himself how to produce Northwest Coast art, then he taught others, including Indian carvers. He briefly assisted in the development of the 'Ksan style of Northwest Coast art at Hazelton, British Columbia, for example, which is an amalgam of traditional and anthropologically reconstructed rule-based principles. It was, in fact, in 1966, the year Codere's prophetic statement was published, that Bill Holm took his slides and notes to Hazelton and lectured there on the elements of Northwest Coast flat design. The codifications produced by Boas and Holm provide the primary criteria according to which the Northwest Coast artist is judged. Indian carvers themselves learn from the Boas and Holm books, and teach from them.

The second way anthropologists contributed to the reconstruction of the meaning of Northwest Coast Indian art was to promote a change in classification, from the exotic status of "primitive art", where it was compared to other tribal and curio traditions, to the more dignified status of "fine art", where it is now compared with the great traditions held in highest esteem by western civilization. Lévi-Strauss was perhaps the first anthropologist to propose this redefinition, writing in 1943 that "certainly the time is not far distant when the collections of the Northwest Coast will move from anthropological museums to take their place in art museums among the arts of Egypt, Persia, and the Middle Ages. For this art is not unequal to those great ones" (1943: 175).

On the west coast since the 1950s a number of people, through their teachings, writings, and exhibits, also promoted this theme of Northwest Coast Indian crafts as fine art. Wilson Duff, who was curator of anthropology at the British Columbia Provincial Museum (BCPM) and then a professor of anthropology at the University of British Columbia, played an especially important role. And one of the more significant exhibits during this period was the 1967 "Arts of the Raven" at Vancouver Art Gallery, curated by Doris Shadbolt, with the assistance of Wilson Duff, Bill Holm, and Haida artist Bill Reid.

In the catalogue prepared for that show, Doris Shadbolt (1967) referred to the "shift in focus from ethnology to art" that the exhibit represented. And eight years later, looking back upon that exhibit, Duff wrote that "Arts of the Raven" was the "threshold over which Northwest Coast art has come into full recognition as 'fine art' as well as 'primitive art'" (1975:13).

In the catalogue Duff prepared for his spectacular exhibition of prehistoric stone sculpture, "Images: Stone: B.C." (1975:24-25), he remarked upon the high intellectual and aesthetic quality of Northwest Coast art With the Images exhibition, he stated, we are at last beginning to grant to the Northwest Coast "artist philosophers" of long ago "credence as people of intellect and mature wisdom." In his words: "to the existing proof of the prior claim and Indian presence in Canada may be added, however poorly understood, this evidence of thirty centuries of hard thinking".

There is by now a well established litany repeated by anthropologists and others on appropriate occasions In his foreword to the 1977 Graphics Collection of the Northwest Coast Indian Artists' Guild, for example, George MacDonald of the National Museum of Man stated that Northwest Coast art, "is only now being internationally acclaimed by experts as of similar importance to the artistic heritage of mankind as are the arts of ancient Egypt and China." William Taylor, director of the National Museum of Man, contributing a foreword to the 1978 Graphics Collection of the Northwest Coast Indian Artists' Guild, observed that Northwest Coast Indian art is "one of mankind's great artistic achievements ranking with the outstanding traditions of China and Japan, tribal Africa, pre-Columbian Middle America and the European Renaissance." He then repeated Lévi-Strauss's proclamation that Northwest Coast art can be placed "on a par with that of Greece and Egypt" (Taylor 1978).

This attempt to redefine and upgrade the meaning of Northwest Coast Indian art, and especially its present representations, has not by any means received universal acceptance. Not everyone has agreed to remove it from the category of primitive or curio art. To give just one example, the Northwest Coast Indian Artists' Guild asked the Vancouver Art Gallery if the Guild's first graphics collection, issued in 1977, could open at the Gallery. The Indian artists, of course, wanted to proclaim to all the message that their silkcreens were "fine art" deserving exhibition in a major art gallery. The Vancouver Art Gallery agreed to have the opening, but hung the prints in an antechamber to its gift shop, through which people had to go in order to see them. The only Gallery staff at the opening were the gift shop manager and her sales clerks there to sell the prints.

2. The Promotion and Legitimation of Indian Art and Artists through Patronage

Museums in British Columbia, especially the three big ones (British Columbia Provincial Museum, University of British Columbia Museum of Anthropology, and Vancouver Centennial Museum) have in the last twenty years been major patrons of contemporary Indian artists. These museums provided or arranged a number of major commissions which helped to establish the legitimacy of contemporary carvers. Probably the single most important event was in 1949 when Audrey and Harry Hawthorn of the UBC Museum of Anthropology commissioned Kwagiutl carvers Ellen Neel and Mungo Martin to restore some of the poles at the university. This commission established Martin as a full-time carver and informant in residence, first for two years at UBC and subsequently for ten years at the Provincial Museum with Wilson Duff. It demonstrated publicly that an honourable living could be made by producing high quality carvings for White people and their museums. (It is interesting to note at this point, and I will discuss it again later, that Duff's successor at the British Columbia Provincial Museum, Peter Macnair, has since endeavoured to demonstrate that carvers can now also make an honourable living by carving once again for Indians.)

After Mungo Martin came Bill Reid and Douglas Cranmer, both commissioned to design and construct Haida houses and poles for the UBC Museum of Anthropology from 1957 through to 1963, and Henry Hunt and his sons (relatives of Martin) at the Provincial Museum in Victoria. The Haida house project was a major one for both Reid and Cranmer. It not only had a considerable influence on their own careers, but it attracted wide attention and influenced others as well. Through the 1960's and 1970's commissions multiplied as did the number of carvers who emerged to take advantage of them. Newly carved totem poles now dot the B.C. landscape and have become a standard gift item for other nations. And during the last ten years carvers have begun to carve and erect poles in their own villages as well. Even Indians are now beginning to collect Indian souvenir art.

In the twenty-four years from 1956 to 1980 the major museums and galleries in British Columbia (BCPM, Vancouver Art Gallery, Vancouver Centennial, UBC), occasionally with the assistance of their gift shops, have produced over thirty temporary exhibitions of Northwest Coast Indian art and opened two major permanent exhibitions (Provincial Museum and UBC), all of which promoted the aesthetic merit of Northwest Coast Indian art, and most of which included contemporary examples (see Table 1). The first important show of this kind was the Audrey Hawthorn and J.A. Morris 1956 "People of the Potlatch" at the Vancouver Art Gallery. Other exhibits that had a major impact were the 1967 "Arts of the Raven"; the 1969 Northwest Coast exhibit at Montreal's Man and His World by the Museum of Anthropology; the 1971 "Legacy"; the 1974 "Bill Reid Retrospective" (see Table 1); and the series of one-man shows and print exhibits instituted at the UBC Museum of Anthropology in

TABLE 1

Some Exhibitions of Northwest Coast Indian Material Culture Displayed as Art by Major Museums and Galleries in B.C., 1956-80

DATE	EXHIBIT	LOCATION	CURATOR/ ORGANIZATION
1956	People of the Potlatch	VAG	J.A. Morris, A. Hawthorn
1958	100 Years of B.C. Art	VAG	R.M. Hume
1967	Arts of the Raven	VAG	D. Shadbolt
1968-70	Age of Edenshaw	VCM	W. Duff
1969	Mungo Martin Retrospective	?	A. Hawthorn
1969	Henry Speck	New Design	A. Hawthorn
1969-70	The Northwest Coast	Man & His World	A. Hawthorn
1971	Robert Davidson	VCM	Gift Shop
1971	The Legacy	BCPM	P. Macnair
1973-74	Selections from the Lipsett Collection	VCM	L. Maranda
1974	Bill Reid: A Retrospective	VAG	D. Shadbolt
1975	Images: Stone: B.C.	AGGV	W. Duff
1975	Northwest Coast Renaissance	VCM	Gift Shop
1976	Opening of new UBC Museum of Anthropology with Legacy Exhibition		
1976	The Cook Argillite Collection	VCM	Gift Shop
1976-77	B.C. Indian Artists at Work	VCM	L. Maranda
1976	Selections from the Lipsett Collection	VCM	L. Maranda
1977	Opening of the Anthropology Gallery	BCPM	P. Macnair et al
1977	The 'Ksan B Show	VCM	Gift Shop
1977	Roy Vickers: Beginnings	UBCMA	H. Ratner
1977	The Lightbawn Collection	VCM	Gift Shop
1977	Norman Tait, Nishga Carver	UBCMA	H. Ratner
1977	Silver Workshop: NWC Carvers at Work ("Treasures of London")	VCM	R. Watt
1977	NWC Indian Artists Guild 1977 Graphics	VAG	Gift Shop
1978	Joe David	UBCMA	H. Ratner
1978	NWC Indian Artists Guild 1978 Graphics	UBCMA	H. Ratner
1979	NWC Indian Artists 1979 Graphics	UBCMA	H. Ratner
1979	Cycles: The Graphic Art of R. Davidson	UBCMA	M. Halpin H. Stewart
1979	The Evolution of Bill Reid's Beaver Print	UBCMA	Student Exhibit
1980	West Coast & Kwakiutl Graphics	UBCMA	Student Exhibits
1980	Salish Weavers	UBCMA	Student Exhibit
1980	Bent Boxes	UBCMA	Student Exhibits
1980	Legacy II (Edinburgh Festival)	BCPM	P. Macnair

Abbreviations

AGGV	Art Gallery of Greater Victoria	VCM	Vancouver Centennial Museum
BCPM	British Columbia Provincial Museum	UBCMA	UBC Museum of Anthropology
VAG	Vancouver Art Gallery		

1977. The earlier shows featured early pieces along with a small sample from contemporary artists, but gradually the balance has shifted to a preponderance of contemporary works of living artists. The Provincial Museum, for example, commissioned most of the pieces for its two Legacy exhibits.

One of the most powerful statements about the aesthetic merits of traditional Northwest Coast Indian art was made by the new UBC Museum of Anthropology when it opened in May 1976. It would not be unreasonable to say that the Great Hall of massive carvings and the Masterpiece Gallery of the museum stunned the public. This was the first time anywhere that such a wide variety of first class Northwest Coast Indian carvings, ranging in age from 13 to 200 years, were ever collected together and elegantly displayed in one place as "masterpieces of fine art". Art experts did not hesitate to proclaim the earlier sculptures as high art on a plane with the great artistic traditions of the world.

To complement its exhibits of traditional carvings, the Museum of Anthropology immediately instituted a programme of presenting contemporary Indian artists and their works after the fashion of one-man shows of White art produced by art galleries (Macfarlane and Inglis 1977; Macfarlane 1978; Halpin 1979).

In 1976 the British Columbia Provincial Museum opened its Anthropology Gallery, and that same year the Museum of Man in Ottawa opened its Children of the Raven Gallery, both of which again played on the theme of fine art. Also in recent years the Vancouver Centennial Museum, especially through its gift shop, has promoted contemporary Indian artists, holding shows for Robert Davidson, Tony Hunt and his colleagues, and 'Ksan. Indian art shows are now a regular occurrence among commercial galleries in Vancouver and Victoria, which suggests that contemporary Indian art is becoming well established in local circles.

What the public museums are in effect doing through their exhibits and acquisitions is to museumify the contemporary Indian artist and his works, and this has the effect of legitimating both artist and artefact in the eyes of both Whites and Indians. Whites see artefacts displayed in museum contexts as collectibles and investments. Indians discover a new value for their own material heritage, seeing what were once stage props now treated as valued objects, sanctified through being coveted by curators, lovingly cared for by professional conservators, and elaborately displayed by artistic designers. Even the carver himself gets displayed and labelled as modern artist. At the UBC Museum of Anthropology, for example, Indian carvers are hired to lecture to students and to the public and arrangements are made for them to be interviewed by the art critics.

3. The Redefinition of the Anthropologist and the Role of Museums

The third way museum anthropologists have influenced the Indian art scene has grown out of their redefinition of the museum enterprise itself. Some museum anthropologists are inverting the relationship between anthropology and the Indian.

In contrast to the traditional role of museums, which was to collect from Indians to show to Whites, this new role involves collecting from Whites to show to Indians. A striking example is provided by the efforts of the British Columbia Provincial Museum and the National Museum of Man to compete in high-priced international art markets to purchase and repatriate to Canada prized pieces of earlier manufacture (Bruce 1976). Another example is provided by the Ethnology Division of the British Columbia Provincial Museum. This division has drawn upon Indian resources to prepare exhibits for the museum's galleries, in the manner that museums have traditionally done. In addition, however, the division has become more and more involved in drawing upon its own resources to cater to the cultural needs of Indian communities. Provincial Museum anthropologists have become the clients and the Indians the patrons, though the anthropologists (or more correctly, their institution) continue to pay the bill.

Here are two examples initiated by the Ethnology Division of the Provincial Museum:

(1) Ever since Kwagiutl master carver Mungo Martin joined the British Columbia Provincial Museum in 1952, Indian carvers have been employed to carve in residence, both to copy museum pieces and to experiment on their own. Ten to twenty years ago, museums in B.C. were concerned about assisting the growth of white markets for these carvings. In more recent years, however, Peter Macnair, Chief Curator of Ethnology at the B.C. Provincial Museum, has also attempted to stimulate an Indian market. He paid his carvers to produce pieces for Indian potlatches, and he has both loaned items from the museum's collection and donated newly carved pieces to sponsors of potlatches. When a few years ago he first invited several young carvers to produce masks for a potlatch, they were sceptical, remarking that it was a rather strange thing to do (personal communication from P. Macnair.) Today, the masks carvers make for potlatches rank among their own most prized possessions (Macfarlane 1978).

(2) The B.C. Provincial Museum Ethnology Division is also putting on tape and film a detailed record of contemporary Kwagiutl potlatching. According to the arrangements worked out by Macnair, the museum acquires custody of the information but ownership remains with the Indians. The museum grants access to scholars only with the permission of the owners, and the owners at no cost to themselves are given photos and copies of the tapes which they use to plan future potlatches or to entertain themselves. (There is also a sign in the Anthropology Gallery of the B.C. Provincial Museum prohibiting the use of tape recorders becau e the songs and music played in the exhibit are "copy righted by Indian families.")

Thus data collected is recycled to the source from which it came, codified electronically and sanctified institutionally perhaps, but recycled nevertheless and without most of it being routed through the traditional scholarly or public audiences of the museum. The British Columbia Provincial Museum Ethnology Division is a leader in providing important cultural services to Indian communities which traditionally were exploited to serve the cultural and economic interests of the others.

Indians, traditionally treated by museums only as objects and clients, add now the role of patrons. The next step has also occurred. Indian communities establish their own museums, seek their own National Museum grants, install their own curators, hire their own anthropologists on contract, and call for the repatriation of their own collections (Inglis 1978). (One notes here the irony of contemporary anthropology: the more widely Indians accept the anthropological definition of their former greatness, the less willing they are to accept the anthropologists themselves. Anthropologists are taking on the second class role among Indians that Indians have always held among Whites. But that is another story.)

Conclusion

Graburn (1968) says that the production of ethnic art in rapidly changing situations functions as an identity-maintaining mechanism for the subject population. What is happening on the Northwest Coast is the active participation of museums and their anthropologists in defining that ethnic identity and the ways it is to be promoted. Anthropologists sit in judgment about what constitutes a proper artefact, a proper price, a proper potlatch and, by implication, a proper Indian.

Meanwhile, Indian communities in cooperation with established museums are beginning to develop their own museum ideologies and to establish their own museumification programmes. Both anthropologists and Indians extol the moral and museological virtues of repatriation of museum collections and of staged authenticity in displays and programmes. It would seem that for some people at least the line between museum anthropologist and Indian has blurred; each is acculturating to the standard of the other. Some anthropologists even carve and dance at potlatches. Museum anthropologists are thus helping to manufacture the objects they study. But this is hardly a new phenomenon. Anthropologists have always been in the business of reconstructing by means of their own theoretical categories the social constructions of those they study. It is not surprising that material culture should receive the same treatment. Nor would it be surprising if we discovered that anthropologists working in other areas are also engaged in the same creative process of helping to create what they set out to study.

NOTES

An earlier version was read at a session on "Museum Ethnology" at the 6th Annual Meeting of the Canadian Ethnology Society, Banff, Canada, February 24, 1979, and was subsequently revised and published in *B.C. Studies*, No. 49, 1981, under the title, "Museum Anthropologists and the Arts of Acculturation on the Northwest Coast." Grateful acknowledgement is made to Carole Farber, Marjorie Halpin, B. Ann Krahn, Peter Macnair and Lynn Maranda for generously providing information for this paper. The author is alone responsible for any errors and omissions, however. It is reprinted here with the permission of the Editors of *B.C. Studies*.

6

De-Schooling the Museum

A Proposal to Increase Public Access to Museums and Their Resources[1]

How can museums make themselves more useful, particularly in rapidly-changing societies? This was the theme of the 13th International Conference of the International Council of Museums, which met in London in July and August, 1983. The ICOM Council indicated that the answer may *not* be found by copying the classical idea of museums as it developed in Europe and North America. Something new is needed.

I would like to suggest a new approach to museum organization, borrowing from the concept of "de-schooling" put forward by Ivan Illich over ten years ago (Illich 1971). The relevance of museums in contemporary society, it is suggested, likely will be determined by the degree to which they are democratized; that is to say, the extent to which there is increasing and more widespread participation in decision-making regarding administration, educational programming, and collections management in museums, and increased opportunities for independent thought and action in cultural matters.[2]

The democratization of administration includes giving those administered a greater say in the organization and conditions of their own work.

The democratization of education includes reducing the role of educational intermediaries and increasing opportunities for independent and individual learning.

The democratization of collection management includes making collections more accessible to the users.

The traditional museum as it developed in Europe and North America began as an elitist institution designed to limit access to the privileged classes. Though museums today serve a much wider clientele, they still retain many exclusive features. Most large museums, for example, grant public access to only a small percentage of their total collection—usually one to five per cent or less—and those objects that are made accessible are usually presented within the context of elaborate interpretations. Access is consequently, in the typical case, highly structured, predetermined, and controlled by museum professionals so as to be "correct," "safe," "understandable," and "educational."

The direction of change in museums especially during the past thirty years has been towards increasing democratization and popularization of their operations. Museums now compete to serve wider populations in an increasing number of ways, and to make their collections more accessible and useful to the general public. More space is being devoted to exhibits, exhibits are becoming more elaborate, more temporary exhibits are mounted, more loans are made to other institutions, and more attention is given to repatriating objects that were illegally removed from other countries. All these strategies enhance the popular function of museums, though they are frequently costly to maintain, they still grant access to only limited parts of the total collections, and they continue to serve only special segments of the general population (see Kelly 1982).

Museum visitor surveys repeatedly show that museums cater almost exclusively to the more highly educated classes. Even though museum attendance may have increased over the past 50 years it is more likely because the level of education has increased than because museums are catering to a broader spectrum.

Until recently the attempts to make museums more accessible have been limited to improving physical access and facilities and to constructing elaborate exhibits (Cameron 1982:179). Collections and the ideas associated with them were being "edited down" to the "lowest common denominator" (ibid., p. 180), "What arrogance," Duncan Cameron, one of Canada's senior museum administrators, wrote recently (ibid.): "What arrogance to assume that we serve our visitors by offering intellectual access to less, not more, and the less to be of our expert choosing." Museums were committed to democratization, Cameron continued, but "we saw improved orientation and interpretation as primary means to that end without realizing that we might be showing the visitors a superb menu and wine list without allowing him to come to the feast."

Another form of democratization that is gaining momentum, one which is both simpler to execute and more radical in its implications, is the idea of increasing direct access to the collections and intellectual resources of the museum, principally by making the museum storage areas themselves open to the public. In some respects this represents an updated version of the older style of museum that displayed row after row of specimens, but it is quite a departure from the norm today. Does open storage help to make a museum more relevant or useful to the community?

I would like to describe examples of accessible storage developed recently in the western part of Canada, and to discuss some of the problems they pose. Their attempts to increase public access are far from perfect, but they should at least provide a basis for further discussion. Other examples could be added. How useful these examples will be as models for rapidly-changing societies is something to be determined. It is at least evident that the type of storage system adopted by a museum—relatively closed or open—has implications for more than public and scholarly access. The choice is likely to be related to how people conceptualize the proper role of museums and how knowledge should be constructed and disseminated.

1. Visible Storage in a University Museum: The University of British Columbia Museum of Anthropology

The first case study is the University of British Columbia Museum of Anthropology's system of "visible storage," which was introduced in 1976 (Ames 1977). As a teaching museum associated with Canada's second largest university, it was considered desirable for the Museum of Anthropology to increase access to teaching collections as much as possible. Thus a system of open or visible storage was devised whereby relatively non-light sensitive objects were arranged in locked glass-fronted cases in a series of galleries open to the public. Books containing computer printout sheets for all the objects were provided as well. The system operates like a large library or supermarket, with the exception that customers can handle objects only under staff supervision; meanwhile, they have unhindered visual access to collections and to the catalogue data.

Interpretive and artistic exhibits are installed elsewhere in the museum, while teaching labs are placed adjacent to the visible storage galleries.

Most of the clothing, textiles, prints, and other light-sensitive objects in the collection are not included in visible storage. A separate, less accessible study-storage system is being designed for these materials (Ames 1981a; Lambert 1983).

The Museum of Anthropology visible storage system works reasonably well for students and scholars, the groups for whom it was primarily designed. It is less successful as a popular entertainment, since it requires effort and some degree of knowledge on the part of the visitor to use the data books, which are not very informative in any case. Security has been improved by installing more secure locking devices and a closed-circuit TV surveillance system. Lighting has been modified by the use of filters (Clavir 1982/83), but lux levels are still high. (To reduce costs, fluorescent tubing was installed at the top of the shelf units, so that high objects receive more light than lower-placed objects.) Most of these problems probably could have been avoided by using more elaborate cabinets, lighting, and computer-assisted information systems, had there been sufficient funds.

2. Visible Storage Adapted to a Community Museum: The Port Alberni Experiment.[3]

When visible storage was adapted to a small community museum in Port Alberni, British Columbia, a town of 20,000 people, it initiated a high degree of visitor participation. The museum opened an enlarged facility in March 1983 that included three public galleries: one featuring artefacts from local Indian communities; a second, about twice the size, holding historical materials from local European settlers, the "pioneers"; and a third small gallery designated for temporary exhibitions. The first two galleries are arranged in a modified visible storage mode which combines, the Alberni director explained (Mitchell 1983),

> public access to collections normally held in out-of-bounds storage areas with a simplified popular catalogue format. A series of interpretive orientation displays weave through the total gallery/storage area to guide the visitor.

Alberni Museum staff report that local visitors were especially intrigued by the catalogue system because they often knew the objects or the previous owners personally, and therefore were able to offer their own additional knowledge and thus related directly and personally with the objects. Open storage in the context of this small town thus becomes an opportunity for members of the community to collectively participate in the recovery and documentation of their own history. Artefacts and catalogue sheets serve as memory releasers and discussion guides, and the museum staff serve as recorders. The museum merges into the community of which it is a part. The level of public participation is apparently high and enthusiastic, though the continued success of this program will also require high levels of public involvement by museum staff, something workers in larger museums usually try to avoid. There is also the question of whether a small collection in a community museum can provide lasting interest, or will the novelty eventually wear off?

3. Stratified Storage at a Large Urban Museum: The Glenbow Project.[4]

The third example is an experiment in study/storage now being conducted by a large urban museum in western Canada, the Glenbow-Alberta Institute in Calgary, the fourth or fifth largest museum of history and art in the country.

Duncan Cameron, the director of the Glenbow, has already written about this project (1982, 1983), and I draw upon his work.

The collections in public museums, Cameron reminds us, are held in trust for the public, and the public, therefore, has a right to have optimum access to those collections and what is known about them (Cameron 1982:179): "...the museum resource, for the visitor, must be a resource designed for access to the museum's totality—its collections, what is known about them, and the human resources of the museum—its curators and educators—whose mandate is to make those collections meaningful and intellectually valuable by every available means."

Access, Cameron continues, means not only physical access to objects but also intellectual access to information about those objects, including, where necessary, curatorial decoding and interpretation. It is to be a stratified access, however, limited and controlled by the specific requirements of particular collections, and by the intellectual interests of the visitor populations. Access is thus organized according to levels of increasing density of collections combined with decreasing levels of interpretation. First is the didactic exhibit where "levels of interpretation (are) at their highest and the density of collection material is probably at its lowest" (Cameron 1982:187). The second level would be publicly-accessible study collections, and the third level with the highest density of artefacts and minimal labelling, would be controlled access to reserve collections. Strategically located between these three levels would be education resource centres, study areas, and curatorial offices.

The principle of stratified access is to provide graduated access to collections and information, "working from an introduction and the creation of interest to the exploration of study collections and, for those with the curiosity and desire, access to the human resources for serious study and research" (ibid.).

The location of curatorial staff represents an important departure from traditional museums that tend to isolate them from the public and the public galleries. In the Glenbow plan, curatorial staff would be placed "in a central position so that they have total command over the collections for which they are responsible..." (ibid.), and would be on occasions accessible as well to the public.

The storage cabinets would be modular and "designed to accommodate everything from large clear spaces to open shelving and systems of drawers of varying proportions operating both vertically and horizontally" (1982:189).

Information would be provided in didactic orientation exhibits, through computer terminals keyed to catalogue numbers of artefacts in accessible storage, in education resource centres, and ultimately by curatorial staff approached through appointments.

Glenbow is now preparing a prototype of the system, using its Western North American ethnology collections, to test it in use. A stratified approach, with individually designed cabinets, micro-environments, and integrated information resources assisted by a computer system, would appear to resolve many of the criticisms levelled against other open storage systems. The Glenbow model is a more expensive system to create and to operate, however, and the division of collections into didactic exhibits, accessible storage, and controlled storage may pose problems of artefact selection, assignment, and management. It also gives curatorial staff a more prominent screening or mediating role than do the other visible storage alternatives.

Conclusions[5]

One way to increase the relevance of museums is to increase public access to the collections and information they contain, so people can become more familiar with the full range of their heritage. It is important for a population placed at risk because of rapid change to have "access to its past, to its traditions, to its culture in order to move into the future" (Appell 1980: 14). People are then more able to "evaluate their past positively and link up the past meanings of life, the past goals and purposes, with the evolving new life, with the evolving new purposes and goals, so that social change can be accomplished more productively, more creatively, and without...painful dislocations" (ibid)

Three types of accessible storage were considered: one designed for a teaching museum at a university, a second adapted to the needs of a small community, and a third being developed for a major urban museum. Other museums are also considering ways of making their collections more accessible, for example Canada's National Museum of Man, New York's Metropolitan Museum of Art, and the British Museum of Science. There are three main criticisms raised against the idea of accessible storage:

1. It is said to expose collections to increased environmental and security risks;
2. it is said to make it difficult to properly interpret the objects (because so many are displayed); and
3. it undermines the responsibilities and authority of the curatorial staff.

The first two problems are essentially mechanical in nature and can be resolved by making use of modern technology. Light, humidity, air purity, and security all can be controlled in a variety of ways, and computer-assisted techniques can be used to increase information flow. How far a museum can go towards resolving these mechanical problems is mostly dependent on how much money it has at its disposal. The Port Alberni experiment demonstrates, however, that low-budget solutions are viable for certain purposes.

The third problem—the change in the responsibilities of curatorial staff brought about by accessible storage—is a different matter. People are more difficult to change than are mechanical systems, and it is apparent that accessible storage threatens some of the prerogatives and assumptions of the curatorial profession.

According to a popular view in museum circles, a museum should interpret or explain carefully-chosen specimens, and "preserve" the bulk of its collections in restricted storage. Various reasons are given as to why artefacts should not be seen without the expert's interpretation: because it is a museum's mission to educate, because the public is believed to need guidance or to not be interested in uninterpreted objects in large collections, or because recreating the original context of the objects helps to justify, or to pay for, the fact that they were removed from their cultural context in the first place. To fail to create a cultural context within a museum exhibition is to commit the crime of "decontextualization," or worse, a blasphemy against the culture from which the objects were obtained.

To give a more concrete idea of the type of objections levelled against accessible storage, I report a number of attitudes recently attributed to staff members of a large North American museum who were engaged in planning a new multi-million dollar facility for their institution:

1. Open storage confuses the visitor. "A person would go crazy in there." The first reaction would be boredom, seeing hundreds of axes or pipes when one would be enough. Then a kind of disorientation,

leaving the visitor exhausted and none the wiser.

2. Through visible storage the museum staff avoid their responsibility to the visitor. It is the duty of the museum staff to present exhibits of the finest materials in their possession, arranged in an appealing and educational fashion. Just dumping all the collections out into the galleries is a basic negation of the museum's role. Many of the museum's collections were never meant for display, are only for study, and should never be inflicted on the general public.
3. Visible storage is an invasion of staff privacy. The work place in the museum, storage, is a private place where the public have no business. Nobody wants to have people looking over their shoulder before they are ready. Open storage ultimately raises the possibility of all the staff working behind glass. The collections are the work place of the museum staff and the idle curiosity of the public has no right there.
4. Who wants open storage anyway? Is there any real evidence that the public want to have it or have asked for it? It seems that the whole idea has been pushed by the education section of the museum. They always say everyone wants it but never give any evidence. It looks like by putting everything out in visible storage they will have to play a greater role in interpretation. Where does that leave the curatorial people? Are education staff going to take over the collections?

One of the consequences of the increasing professionalization of museum work is that members of this developing profession begin to consider it their special responsibility and privilege to control and structure the relations between collections and the public, as the attitudes cited above suggest. Curatorial staff who hold this view present themselves as the necessary agents not only for the care but also for the interpretation of heritage, just as teachers consider their curricula a necessary condition for learning (Illich 1971). They see it as their responsibility to structure the experience of the visitor, principally by means of didactic or text-book exhibits which they assume—though there is little evidence—are effective instruments for conveying knowledge.

The view that favours wider access to collections, on the other hand, is more likely to be associated with ideas about "de-schooling" the museum enterprise, by lessening rather than increasing institutional arrangements between object and viewer (Rowan 1978). Museum exhibits create artificial and stereotyped contexts that may obscure the objects they are intended to feature (Halpin 1978). Access to heritage, according to this view, is a democratic right, and that means access to the objects themselves and to information about those objects (catalogue data) in addition to, perhaps even instead of, pre-packed curatorial interpretations. Museum visitors are to be encouraged to pursue their own investigations as well through independent learning, with various aids to be provided by the museums such as computer terminals, small introductory exhibits, and the occasional availability of curatorial staff serving as resource people or "librarians."

It appears that attitudes towards storage techniques are linked to more deeply felt notions about the role and use of knowledge in society, such as the extent to which knowledge should be structured and mediated by professionals or liberated from institutional interpretations.

If museums wish to improve their social utility then they might consider sharing more of their collections and intellectual resources with the community. As long as access is restricted to structured and interpreted exhibits, which is now the prevailing custom in North American and European museums, then museums will cater only to the interests of those few among the educated strata who seek out formal learning or tourist experiences (Kelly 1982). The more museums can democratize their operations and increase public access to their resources, the more likely they will appeal to wider audiences. Access can be enhanced by improving physical facilities; and it can be further enhanced by opening up the storerooms and making catalogue data available so people can explore beyond the one to five per cent of the collections curators arbitrarily decide the public should see.

Museums can also learn how to increase their usefulness by observing successful operations in the commercial sector. Take as one example the mass marketing of furniture by a company called Ikea. The firm originated in Sweden and has become quite successful in Canada, where it offers convenient supermarket style shopping facilities for people seeking medium cost furniture. Perhaps there are ideas in examples like this for museums to consider, ideas about how to make visitors comfortable and how to display as much as possible in meaningful but not heavily interpreted ways so visitors can explore and experiment according to their individual interests.

NOTES

1. Ranchi University, January 1984. An earlier version of this paper was presented to the International Committee of Architecture and Museum Techniques of the International Council of Museums, London, August 1983.

2. I limit my remarks to museums of history, culture and art because they are more familiar to me.

3. I would like to thank John Mitchell, director, and Nathalie Macfarlane, curator, of the Port Alberni Museum for their assistance in obtaining information about their programme.

4. I would like to thank Duncan Cameron, Director of the Glenbow Museum, for his assistance in obtaining information about the Glenbow experiment.

5. Grateful acknowledgement is made to Stephen Inglis for information that assisted in the writing of this conclusion.

7

Are Museums or Anthropology Really Necessary Any More?

Some years ago, Dr. Wilcomb Washburn, a senior curator at the Smithsonian Institution in Washington, DC, asked if museums were necessary any more (Washburn 1968:1):

> I ask seriously whether, in the future, the museum object will not be converted into information that is as satisfactory for human purposes as the object itself. Should this occur, will it be necessary to preserve the object, let alone exhibit it? ... The object, removed from its context, distorted by the ravages of time and environment, can, conceivably, be a less accurate statement of itself than a description accurately recorded and readily available.

Social and cultural anthropologists—henceforth I will follow the museum tradition and refer to them as ethnologists—are not asking whether they are necessary. They like to assume that they are, of course. But they are asking about the future of the profession. "Where are we heading?", Richard Preston asks (1983:294) in his review of the social structure of Canadian anthropology. We are heading towards a crisis, "we are being challenged from many sides all at once," states Marc-Adélard Tremblay, one of Canada's most distinguished anthropologists, in a paper published in the same volume as Preston's review (Tremblay 1983:332). (For similar laments in reference to United States anthropology, see Hoebel, Currier, and Kaiser 1982.)

The discipline of anthropology, according to Tremblay, "is undergoing a serious crisis that threatens its foundations by calling into question its traditional objectives" (ibid.). It is a crisis facing science as a whole:

> Can we claim that anthropology has achieved the scientific objectives of its founding members? It has been incapable of demonstrating its utility either to client communities or to bureaucratic power brokers, be they in government, in large public corporations or in private business. The crisis of anthropology has multiple facets and far-reaching consequences. It comes at a time of unprecedented theoretical fragmentation, when a confusing plethora of new methodologies are competing to be the anthropological breakthrough to the new science. In the meantime, programmes in action anthropology are coming to a halt because of the questioning of the ultimate objectives of such endeavours and because the quest for knowledge has relied not only on scientific premises but also on ideological paradigms (Tremblay 1983:333).

To make matters worse, as if we needed to, university enrolment in Canada is expected to decline by about 20 per cent over the next ten years because of the drop in the birth rate that followed the post-second world war baby boom (Siminovitch 1979: 11, 18), and this most certainly will lead to a reduction in academic opportunities for anthropologists as well as for others.

There are about 300 to 400 ethnologists practicing in Canada today, most holding positions in 35 universities across the country and others in museums or private practice (Burridge 1983: 307). Burridge works that out to one ethnologist for every 90,000 people in the country, compared to one per 80,000 in the United States, one to 330,000 in the United Kingdom, and one to 120,000 in Australia (ibid.). No growth potential here.

Where, indeed, is Canadian ethnology heading, and is the situation much different anywhere else in the western world? The newsletter for the American Anthropology Association reported in its September 1983 issue that "over 40 per cent of anthropology doctorate recipients were still seeking employment at the time the doctorate was completed," the highest percentage for all major fields and a dramatic increase over the twelve per cent registered ten years previously (American Anthropology Association 1983:4).

Questions are being asked with increasing frequency. Are museums really necessary any more? Does ethnology serve any useful purpose that could not now be more effectively performed by other disciplines, such as sociology, geography or economics? Who needs ethnology besides the ethnologists themselves? Is any part of anthropology now relevant, science writer Christopher Hallowell asked in an article recently published in the journal of the US Public Broadcasting Communications System (1983: 46):

> ...social psychology and sociology, anthropology's nearest relatives, regularly hit much closer to home. Scientists in those fields tell us how we can best get through life. They tell us how we deal with stress, what effect urban life has on us, and how scared we all are. They tell us about the effects of long-distance plane travel on our bodies and minds, which seems a bit more pertinent than learning (from an anthropological study) how stewardesses behave on planes.

The popular attitude towards anthropology is even more negative, though much of this criticism is directed towards the very idea of social science which, in the typical case, is accused of providing academically obscure interpretations of the obvious and the ordinary. As one outspoken critic, a retired magistrate who now writes a column in a daily newspaper in Vancouver, Cana a, recently put it (Bewley 1983):

> ...an anthropologist, sociologist, psychologist, political scientist, or criminologist can for generations peddle, without being caught out, absurd and downright disastrous ideas about education, child-rearing, human relationships, government, and the reformation of crooks.
>
> With his fool ideas it is possible for him to ruin several generations of citizens and their families, destroy their peace of mind and their safety on the streets, and bankrupt national treasuries. By the time the facts catch up with and expose the catastrophic consequences of his teachings, the silly blighter has been appointed a professor emeritus and is too honoured, too white-haired, too old and too feeble, to be tarred and feathered and run out of town on a rail.

Fortunately, there are some encouraging responses to these challenges. Surely museums are necessary since so many new ones are built and old ones renovated every year. "No statement about an object is as complete a statement about the object as the object itself", Washburn (1968:1) of the Smithsonian said, so there will be a continuing need for museums to collect, preserve, research and exhibit specimens. The more rapidly traditional crafts disappear along with the tribal populations that made and used them, the more important it is for museums to rescue some of the evidence.

It is becoming more widely recognized now that one of the important roles museums perform is to serve as symbols of status and prestige (Kelly 1983). Visiting an important museum is a highly acceptable and socially visible way of validating and demonstrating one's status in the community. According to social psychologist Robert Kelly (1983), who has been examining the status role of museums, a growing number of people who visit such institutions do so "to attain a state of *having been there*" (emphasis in the original).

Museums have become the temples and palaces of modern society, expressing in contemporary idiom—through both their architecture and their contents—the essential values of the community (Mayer 1979: 130), which thus makes it possible for them to perform their "status-conferring" role (Kelly 1983: 12). Museums also serve as political instruments of the state, for example, national museums which are expected to present the authorized or established picture of a nation's history and culture or to serve as monuments to the benevolence and culture of the governing party itself (see Dickson's 1983 discussion of France's plans for a monumental new science museum in Paris). A large museum of art is a necessary part of a city's image of sophistication. When the art gallery in Vancouver, Canada, recently moved into a newly renovated old building, for example, the city celebrated as if it had finally come of age. This move to the impressive old building with its modern renovations, the local newspaper proclaimed (McMartin 1983), "places the city (of Vancouver) on an equal footing with the best the country has to offer."

It took four evenings to celebrate the opening of the new Vancouver Art Gallery, with crowds of excited people each evening. The first to come were members of the local establishment, the city's elite, who rolled up in Rolls-Royces, Mercedes, Jaguars, BMWs, and Cadillac limousines, parking on lawns and sidewalks with "bravado", the local newspaper reported (McMartin 1983), "where only the rich and powerful would dare." Five hundred guests in formal attire attended on that first night, paying $250 each for champagne, dinner and a string orchestra. The more ordinary members of the public visited the newly-opened gallery during the next three days, for the first two of those three days by invitation only and on the last day everyone else who was left over and still interested.

For the first time in Vancouver's history, the local newspaper said (Johnson 1983), the city will have a "real art gallery." What is a "real" art gallery? Vancouver actually has had an art gallery for over 50 years, but until this move it was lodged in an ordinary building. It now has a facility of monumental stature, though the quality of its collections remain the same as before. A real art gallery, a newspaper reporter explained

(Johnson 1983):

> is a gallery in a gracious and dignified building. A real art gallery displays entirely too much for anyone to see and absorb in one visit. A real art gallery provides that delightful experience, hitherto available only in more sophisticated urban centres, of visual overload.

Small towns want their museums and galleries as well, to preserve and display their own local histories and their own arts and crafts. Every self-respecting community needs a museum to contribute to that sense of self-respect. The more a modern society removes itself from its past, and sees change as "coterminous with progress" and innovation as "coterminous with improvement" (Shils 1981:4), the more the past is reduced to nostalgic memories and people feel they need museums to store their nostalgia, those beliefs and values which, though they are still much admired, no longer serve as models for the future (Shils 1981: 3).

Do museums play a significantly different role in those societies that continue to draw upon their past traditions as normative models for future action? What happens when a museum attempts to "museumify" living traditions? The Special Committee on Antiquities in Sri Lanka described just such a problem in its final report published in 1959 (Special Committee on Antiquities 1959: 17. Quoted in Bandara 1972:53):

> Archaeology in Ceylon has of necessity; to deal with the remains of religious edifices that pertain to two living religions—Buddhism and Hinduism. In this respect archaeological work in Ceylon is beset with certain difficulties that are not found in a country like Egypt or even in certain parts of India. The vast majority of people in Ceylon treat archaeological remains not as historical or scientific curiosities but as sacred sites and buildings. They are only secondarily significant to them as historical or scientific data. The people's wishes and emotions are primarily important, but it is absolutely necessary that a compromise must be found in this matter between the demands of religious fervour and scientific study, for these monuments are priceless and constitute indispensable material to the historian and the archaeologist.

Museum attendance continues to grow, outstripping even—it is claimed—attendance at professional sporting events. So those working in museums can answer loudly and clearly, "Yes, museums are necessary, because the people want them!" But are they necessary for the right reasons? Does the increasing popularity of museums subvert them from their original mission as scholarly institutions, and therefore subvert the work of those employed within? Or, to look at it another way, are those working in museums today, including especially ethnologists, adequately trained for the public roles unfolding upon them? In actual fact ethnologists are not trained for many of the duties they are now expected to perform in contemporary museums and galleries, and that is a problem.

Academic ethnologists are also inclined, naturally, to say that their ethnology is also necessary; but in their case they cannot claim it is because the people want it. On the contrary, to the dismay of the profession, ethnology appears to be declining in popularity, among students, in the general population, and—most embarrassing of all—among those whom ethnologists traditionally study (Lurie 1976). Probably one of the greatest shocks an ethnologist can experience—and it seems to be occurring with increasing frequency—is to have the people one studied read what one wrote about them, and complain both stridently and publicly about misinterpretation and distortion. The personal interpretation the ethnographic technique produces makes ethnologists particularly vulnerable to this kind of criticism.

Under the cirumstances we had better give more serious attention to the state of our profession, Richard Preston warns (1983:294) in his recent article on the structure of Canadian ethnology:

> With a promised decline in university entrance populations, inflation, recession, an ungenerous mood on the part of government and...the populace as far as university support is concerned, we are faced with the fact that the boom is finished, and strategic withdrawals...from the aspirations and expectations of the past decade must come.

What has gone wrong? Museums are more popular than ever, though apparently more as status symbols than as the institutions of research and education their curators prefer. The academic version of ethnology, despite unparalleled growth in numbers and in the sophistication of theories and methodologies (Tremblay 1983), appears to be declining in popularity and public respect. Somehow ethnologists are missing the boat; those in museums grumble about their increasingly public role, while those in Academe lament their declining popularity.

Ethnologists who today work in museums and universities were all trained in a context where the importance of research and the principle of scientific freedom were held to be primary values, transcending even the responsibility to respond to public demands. The foundations for these ideas can be traced back to the Renaissance and the "educational revolution" (Parsons and Platt 1973:3) that followed. Scholars have come to assume that the acquisition and free exchange of knowledge is accepted as common practice throughout the civilized world. "The unhindered opportunity to conduct research, to freely discuss issues and to publish ideas, was seen as central to both the further development of science and to the improvement of human life (Nason 1981: 3). As the process of democratization continues to evolve along its natural course, however, towards expanding the concept of equality to an ever widening range of people and societies—the principle of scientific freedom is also, as it were, subjected to the pressures of democratization.

It is becoming more widely accepted as a characteristic of modern society that the general public has rights to know about and to share in the benefits of scientific knowledge. In concrete terms this means increasing public demands for demonstrable returns on taxpayers' investment in education and research (Manning 1983b; Loubser 1983). Museums, for example, must contend with growing public interest in how they collect and what they do with their collections. As museum anthropologist James Nason put it (1981: 18), "...our ability to freely collect data, along with the notion that research work was an inviolable activity, has diminished in the face of new legal and social conditions." Museums must now be more sensitive to national, ethnic, and local interests, and consider more carefully the prospects of "repatriating" parts of their collections to the ethnic or national communities from which they were originally taken (Inglis 1979).

Given these circumstances, both the inevitable progress of democratic ideas and the continuing reluctance of scholars to give up their traditional academic privileges, how do we answer those questions with which I began? Are museums necessary? Is ethnology still necessary?

The necessity of museums can be justified by reference to their traditional functions of collection, preservation, research, and public education, and to their roles as status symbols, status conferring institutions, and national monuments. Some museums are trying to do more than this, however. Museums are making significant attempts to increase public access to their collections and their intellectual resources, for example. And museums are also beginning to play more active roles in the regeneration and promotion of cultural traditions, especially for those populations subject to high risk because of rapid social change. I will give several examples.

First, the matter of increased public access. It has been characteristic of most large museums in recent years to claim that they serve an educational mission while at the same time following a policy of granting the public access to no more than one to five per cent of their total collections. Items from storage may be rotated with those on display, but only to a minor degree. It is also now customary to present museum objects in a context that is heavily didactic. Specimens are used as visual aids for educational messages. Public access thus means, in the typical case, access to a rigidly limited selection of objects lodged within a highly structured interpretive framework. Visitors cannot make their own selections nor are they encouraged to develop their own interpretations. What is interesting about this mode is the fact that there is little evidence to suggest that it achieves the purpose intended, the moral and educational uplift of the general public. Some museums, therefore, are beginning to question this way of doing things and to explore alternatives.

"Whatever else our museums do well," British museologist Brian Lewis (1980: 151) noted recently, "they most certainly do not provide the general visiting public with a good educational experience." The evidence, in fact, suggests that didactic exhibits are not effective educational instruments. Museum visitors typically stand for no longer than 20 to 40 seconds in any one place, avoid reading most labels in an exhibit, and steadily reduce the attention they devote to exhibits and labels the closer they come to exit signs, a phenomenon referred to as the "exit gradient" (Brown 1978). Whenever the learning outcome of exhibits is measured, the results are erratic and idiosyncratic, "leaving museum personnel with the conviction that something is being acquired, but at the same time being unable to specify or demonstrate what" (ibid., p. 6). Exhibits are rarely compared with other instructional media, but there is no reason to think they would be as effective in conveying information as lectures, textbooks, or audio-visual presentations (One study in Sweden (Arnell *et al.*, 1976: 50), comparing an exhibition with a video tape on the same subject and with similar contents, found the tape to be more effective in conveying knowledge and more preferred by the subjects. The subject group which saw the video tape first and the exhibit afterwards had the highest retention of knowledge, and the group that saw only the exhibit had the lowest.)

Since limited access didactic exhibits are not fulfilling the educational purpose for which they were intended, some museums are considering alternative approaches, including various attempts to "de-school" approaches by reducing formal and didactic exhibitions and programmes and by increasing public access to their collections and information through open storage techniques (Ames 1983b). These museums see themselves operating more as learning centres and cultural resource banks than as annexes to the school system.

Museums are also playing more active roles in the regeneration and promotion of the cultural traditions and social histories of local communities, especially the "populations at risk" who are undergoing rapid social change. In his review of the conflicts and disturbances that result from rapid change, George Appell (1980:14) noted the importance of planning that includes "ethnographic research, the development of museums, the creation of archives that contain the oral literature, song, dance, and art of the population at risk, and the study of its social history and oral traditions." These approaches, Appell continues:

> ...provide the opportunity whereby the members of the population at risk can evaluate their past positively and link up the past meanings of life, the past goals and purposes, with the evolving new life, with the evolving new purposes and goals, so that social change can be accomplished more productively, more creatively...It is important that a population have access to its past, to its traditions, to its culture in order to move into the future.

Successful adjustment to rapid change requires that the past be conceived of as a meaningful and an important experience on which to build. There is an obvious role here for museums to play (Appell 1980).

When I say that museums actively engage in cultural programming for populations at risk, I do not mean simply the promotion of traditional handicrafts and customs as they used to be performed, reconstructed with the assistance of the ethnologist. The purpose is not to preserve craft technologies or tribal customs as living museum curiosities. This is a static view of tribal culture that some museums and ethnologists fostered in the past, perhaps with good intent but to the detriment of the peoples concerned. While it is the business of museums to preserve old artefacts and to recover the past, it is not their business to preserve living peoples in an ethnologically reconstructed image of the past. It is just as natural for artistic and craft traditions, and a peoples' interpretation of their own social history, to evolve over time as it is for language, kinship, or economic patterns. Museums can play a useful role by encouraging experimentation with these traditions, by recording the changes as they occur, and by helping to develop critical standards by which people can judge their experiments with their own cultural forms. Museums could assist, for example, in the introduction of synthetic fibres, the use of power tools and machines, the application of traditional designs to modern media such as limited edition serigraphs or acrylic painting, experimentation with design itself, the development of new cultural performances inspired by traditions and comparison with other styles, and the exploration of new markets for fine arts as well as for inexpensive souvenirs.

It can be said that museums are necessary because of the continuing acceptance of their traditional functions and because of the newer functions they perform, especially for those communities exposed to risk because of rapid social change, by providing increased public access to their collections and intellectual resources and by actively supporting the continuing evolution of crafts, traditions, and cultural performances. What about ethnology outside of museums, however? Is that also necessary?

Ethnologists can always think of uses for ethnology, but the challenge is to convince others. When it is said that the public in a democratic society claims a right to know what is being done with its money, that does not mean research should always serve the public in an immediate and applied sense. It does mean, however, that ethnologists need to communicate more effectively and to larger audiences the significance of what they do if they wish to justify continued public support. "Most anthropologists just don't know how to communicate or don't choose to communicate to the general public," science writer Christopher Hallowell stated (1983:47) in his discussion of the United States television documentary, "Anthropology on Trial" "We need a more interesting insight into their work...."

One way ethnologists can achieve greater public recognition is for themselves to give more recognition to the practical uses of their own discipline. Applied anthropology has a long history, but it is considered by most academics, in North America, at least, to be second class, and consequently is poorly understood and underappreciated (Salisbury 1983:196-7). Perhaps some anthropologists have rejected applied anthropology because of its earlier association with colonialism; it is, nevertheless, one aspect of the discipline that could be readily understood and appreciated by the public.

The opportunities for practical work are immense and are only partly exploited by ethnologists. I will give a few examples.[1] The most common form is applied anthropology in the traditional sense, the "client-sponsored" research that ethnologists perform for others. Studies for colonial administrations, impact assessments for government agencies and private corporations, and historical research for indigenous populations are well known examples. (Reviews of applied research in Canada may be found in Manning 1983a and Weaver 1981.)

Client-sponsored research is also conducted in museums and schools. Anthropologists use ethnographic and survey techniques to assess the performance of particular programmes or exhibits and their subtle or hidden messages (Halpin 1978). Robert Wolf (1980), who is associated with the Smithsonian Museum in Washington, talks about "naturalistic-responsive" evaluation techniques, which are essentially ethnographic ones. Similar methods are now widely used in educational research as well (Guba and Lincoln 1983). "Accountability," Wolf says (1980:39), "is sweeping across the museum world today as it has swept over public, social and cultural institutions during the last decade." Evaluation research has thus become a rapidly growing field and one in which ethnologists are only beginning to make their presence felt.

There are two other kinds of practical anthropology less frequently practised, but possibly more important in the long run both to the profession and to society. The first of these alternative applications is the anthropological study of anthropology itself, a reflexive mode. The principle is a simple one: we study ourselves as we customarily view others, we treat ourselves as if we were the natives. We are our own clients. Examples include studies of recruitment into the profession, how we organize our work, and how we construct our theories (Scholte 1969; Ames 1979, 1981b). The continuing debate in India over what constitutes a proper "Sociology of India" is another good example, and one that ethnologists in other countries would do well to emulate.

Another form of reflexive anthropology is the use of anthropological knowledge and technique in administrative work, a form of "working anthropology". Ethnologists who become administrators usually discover very quickly how their anthropological perspective is useful in eliciting the point of view of the other, in uncovering hidden meanings and background assumptions, in identifying cultural and ethnic nuances, in recognizing symbols of power and authority, in assessing realistic alternatives, and in generating respect for differences of opinion. Anthropologically derived insights directly assist in the making of practical decisions and in weighing the costs and benefits (functions and dysfunctions) of those decisions.

The second alternative application of ethnology is to use it as a form of social criticism. I have in mind here ethnologists in the role of intellectuals who critically interpret their "society and its culture to their own countrymen and the world" (Green 1977: 39), what Laura Nader (1969:293) once referred to as "writing ethnography for the 'natives'" so they have the information they need to improve their lives. "By helping members of a community to comprehend social reality more explicitly and generally," Dell Hymes wrote (1969:54) in his introduction to the book *Reinventing Anthropology*, "one may help people to employ what C. Wright Mills called 'sociological imagination'...and to be in greater control of their own destinies."

Ethnologists could certainly contribute to an understanding of how power and responsibility are exercised in modern societies. Indeed, there is a certain urgency to the kind of anthropology that is concerned with power, Laura Nader observes (Nader 1969:284):

> ...the quality of life and our lives themselves may depend upon the extent to which citizens understand those who shape attitudes and actually control institutional structures. The study of man is confronted with an unprecedented situation: never before have so few, by their actions and inactions, had the power of life and death over so many members of the species.

Social critics, sociologist Ralf Dahrendorf (1970:55) once said, are the "court jesters" of modern society, whose role is "to doubt everything that is obvious, to make relative all authority, to ask all those questions that no one else dares to ask." The task of intellectuals as critics is to voice the uncomfortable as well as comfortable truths about society, and thus to create opportunities for understanding and change.

In 1971, William Burns, then director of the San Diego Natural History Museum, advocated a critical role for museum curators, saying that they should act like canaries (Burns 1971:217). The canary bird was used by underground miners to warn them of noxious fumes before they are overcome. The curator-as-canary serves as an early warning signal for society, informing the general public through the arts about dangers that lie ahead.

The curator-as-canary is the "Curator-with-a-Social-Conscience" (Burns 1971:219), and is in practice as rare a bird as the ethnologist in the role of intellectual court jester. Questioning accepted values and institutions is not a comfortable or popular undertaking, and is frequently subjected to public criticism and ridicule (Dahrendorf 1970). Museums are predisposed more towards a positive view of history than a critical one, in any case. The dinosaurs, aborigines, and pioneers depicted in exhibits are all typically presented as noble creatures who in the distant past struggled heroically but (except for the pioneer European settlers of the New World) ultimately unsuccessfully against the brute forces of nature. Rarely will a museum exhibit imply a criticism of the past or the present, though admittedly it is fashionable in North American museums to present a muted criticism of European pioneers for destroying the traditional cultures of native American Indians. But North American museums would never dare to subject native Indians themselves, or the contemporary establishment, to objective scrutiny or critical assessment. Native people are sacred to museum ethnologists, and are consequently removed from virtually all critical comment. Given the tenuous financial basis of museums it is understandable why they also would shy away from being too critical of mainstream society.

University departments of anthropology, at least in North America, where academic freedom is more protected than in museums, are not much more productive as locations for the critical spirit. Native peoples, especially those living close enough to be reported in the local press or to visit one's office, are equally sacred to academic ethnologists, who want to avoid the embarrassment of being criticized by the people who traditionally served as their subject matter. Academic ethnologists also have not contributed much to the public discussion of social and cultural policies or to the critical assessment of major social institutions, though there are a few notable exceptions (for example, Nader 1980a, 1980b, 1983).

The applied anthropology that has flourished the most is the client-sponsored form. The reflexive and critical versions remain underdeveloped, and they may be the perspectives the most needed. We need more court jesters and canaries.

Over 50 years ago Malinowski (1929) called for a more concentrated effort to bridge the gap between theoretical anthropology and its practical applications, for there existed, he said, an "anthropological no man's land" between the two. Practical people need the knowledge anthropologists can provide, but academic anthropology is dominated by "sensational or antiquarian interests" The anthropologist, said Malinowski, "...still tries to close his eyes to the surrounding reality and reconstructs laboriously a savage who does not exist any more—who, in Melanesia ceased to exist a generation ago, in Africa some two generations ago, and in North America perhaps one hundred years or more" (ibid., p. 37)

That bridge between theory and practice, between academic interests and socially responsive performance, still needs to be constructed if anthropologists hope to convince others of their value and their necessity. Ethnologists working in museums and in universities have a common interest here and could usefully pool their talents in the search for solutions.

Museums continue to be necessary because their social utility continues to be recognized—their traditional functions of collection, preservation, research, education, and status enhancement, and their more recent efforts to serve populations at risk. But what about the profession of anthropology? Is that also necessary? Looking at the condition of the world around us, we can only say "yes" because of the need for the special kind of knowledge anthropologists can provide. But we need to make this knowledge more accessible if we are to make our utility more visible.

NOTES

1. This concluding section is drawn from a paper presented to the First Annual Meeting of the Society for Applied Anthropology in Canada, May 11, 1982, and subsequently published in an Occasional Paper of that Society (Ames 1983a).

Bibliography

Adams, Marie Joanne

1981 Mediating our Knowledge. *In* A.E. Cantwell, J.B. Griiffin, and N.A. Rothschild, eds., *The Research Potential of Anthropological Museum Collections.* Annals of the New York Academy of Sciences 376: 289-300.

Alexander, Edward P.

1979 *Museums in Action: An Introduction to the History and Functions of Museums.* Nashville: American Association of State and Local History.

Alexander, Robin

1981 The Evaluation of Naturalistic, Qualitative, Contextualist, Constructivist Inquiry in Art Education. *Review of Research in Visual Arts Education* 13: 34-43.

American Anthropology Association

1983 Award for Highest 22 of Unemployed PhDs Goes to—Anthropologv *Anthropology Newsletter* 24(6): 6-7.

Ames, Michael M.

1977 Visible Storage and Public Documentation. *Curator* 20 (1): 65-79.

1979 Applied Anthropology in Our Backyards. *Practicing Anthropology* 2 (1): 7, 23-24.

1981a Preservation and Access: A Report on an Experiment in Visible Storage. Canadian Museums Association *Gazette*, Summer-Fall, pp. 22-33.

1981b Museum Anthropologists and the Arts of Acculturation on the Northwest Coast. *B.C. Studies* No. 49, pp. 3-14.

1983a Canaries and Court Jesters: Some Practical Implications of Practicing Anthropology in Museums and Academic Institutions *In* Kathryn T. Molohon, ed., Panel Discussion on the Present State of the Art of

Applied Social Science in Canada. *Occasional Papers of the Society of Applied Anthropology/Societé d'Anthropologie Appliquée du Canada*, No. 1. pp. 3-11.

1983b De-Schooling the Museum: A Report on Accessible Storage for the International Committee of Architecture and Museum Techniques, 13th General Conference of the International Council of Museums, London, July-August, 1983.

Appell, George

1977 The Plight of Indigenous Peoples: Issues and Dilemmas. *Survival International Review* 2 (3): 11-16.

1980 The Social Separation Syndrome. *Survival International Review* 5(1): 13-15.

Arnell, Ulla, and Inger Hammer, Goran Nylof

1976 *Going to Exhibitions.* Stockholm: Riksutstallningar.

Bandara, H.H.

1972 *Cultural Policy in Sri Lanka.* Paris: UNESCO Studies and Documents on Cultural Policies.

Baxi, Smita J.

1973 Museum Exhibitions and Display Techniques. *In* S. J. Baxi and V.P. Dwivedi, *Modern Museum Organization and Practice in India.* New Delhi: Abhinav Publications. pp. 57-84.

Benedict, Burton

1983 *The Anthropology of World's Fairs. San Francisco's Panama Pacific International Exposition of 1915.* London and Berkeley: The Lowie Museum of Anthoropology and Scolar Press.

Bewley, Les

1983 Cancelling the Penalty for Failure. *The Sun* Newspaper, Vancouver, Canada, October 25, p. 5.

Blackwood, Beatrice

1970 Classification of artefacts in the Pitt Rivers Museum Oxford. Occasional Papers on Technology II. Oxford: Pitt Rivers Museum.

Boas, Franz

1907 Some Principles of Museum Administration. *Science,* n.s., 25 (650) 921-33.

1927 *Primitive Art,* Institutet for Sammenlignernde Kulturforskning, Series B. Vol. 8. Oslo (reprinted by Dover Publications in 1955).

Bogaart, N.C.R.

1978 Reality in Motion: Audio-Visuals as a Means of Transmitting Information in Museums. *In* Grace Morley, ed., *Visualization of Theoretical Concepts in Anthropology in Museums of Ethnography.* New Delhi: National Museum of Natural History, pp. 43-47.

Bonner, Alice

1981 Smithsonian Counts Its Treasures — 78 Million or So. *The Sun* Newspaper, Vancouver, Saturday, October 17, p. 3.

Boucher, Pierre

1977 A Museums Policy for Quebec. Canadian Museums Association *Gazette* 10 (3): 54-56.

Britan, Gerald M.

1978a The Place of Anthropology in Programme Evaluation. *Anthropological Quarterly* 51 (2): 119-128.

1978b Experimental and Contextual Models of Program Evaluation. *Evaluation and Program Planning* 1: 229-234.

Brown, Walter S.

1978 The Museum Visitor: Demography and Behavior. Unpublished paper, University of Washington, Seattle, U.S.A.

Bruce, Jean

1976 Reclaiming the History of Canada. *Saturday Night.* June, pp. 29-34.

Bruman, Carol

1982 A 21st Century Walk Through Time. *Maclean's Magazine,* Toronto, September 27, p. 48.

Burns, William A.

1971 The Curator-as-Canary. *Curator* 14 (3): 213-220.

Burridge, Kenelm

1983 An Ethnology of Canadian Ethnology. *In* Manning 1983a. pp. 306-320.

Butler, Barbara H., and Adrienne L. Horn

1983 A Natural Partnership. *Museum News,* August, pp. 42-43.

Cameron, Duncan F.

1971 The Museum, a Temple or the Forum. *Curator* 14 (1): 11-24.

1982 Museums and Public Access: the Glenbow. *International Journal of Museum Management and Curatorship* 1:177-196.

1983 Museums and Public Access. *In* Barry Lord and Gail Dexter Lord, eds., *Planning Our Museums.* Ottawa: National Museums of Canada, pp. 84-102.

Cannizzo, Jean

1979 Historical Myths and Mythical Histories: The View From the Small Museum. Paper presented to the Annual Conference of the Canadian Ethnology Society, Banff, Alberta, Canada,

1982 *Old Images/New Metaphors: The Museum in the Modern World, Parts I-III.* Canadian Broadcasting Corporation Transcripts, "Ideas" Programme. February 21-25.

Clavir, Miriam

1982/83 Notes on Changing Case Lighting. British Columbia Museum *Round-up* 88: 22-23.

Codere, Helen

1966 Introduction, Franz Boas, *Kwakiutl Ethnography*. Chicago: University of Chicago Press,

Collier, Donald, and Harry Tschopik. Jr.

1954 The Role of Museums in American Anthropology. *American Anthropologist* 56: 768-779.

Dahrendorf, Ralf

1970 The Intellectual and Society: The Social Function of the 'Fool' in the Twentieth Century. *In* Philip Rieff, ed., *On Intellectuals: Case Studies.* New York: Anchor Books, pp. 53-56.

Darnell, Regna

1979 The Sapir Years at the National Museum, Ottawa. *In* J. Freedman, ed., *The History of Canadian Anthropology.* Canadian Ethnology Society.

Dickson, David

1983 France's Monumental Science Museum. *Science* 221: 836-838.

Duff, Wilson

1975 *Images Stone B.C.: Thirty Centuries of Northwest Coast Indian Sculp-*

ture. Saanichton: Hancock House Publishers.

Duffek, Karen

1982b "Authenticity" and the Marketing of Contemporary Northwest Coast Indian Art. Paper presented to the Ninth Annual Meeting of the Canadian Ethnology Society, Vancouver. Canada, May 11.

1983a A guide to Buying Contemporary Northwest Coast.

1983b Authenticity and the Contemporary Northwest Coast Indian Art Market. *B.C. Studies* 57: 99-111.

1983c *The Contemporary Northwest Coast Indian Art: The Market Context.* Unpublished M.A. thesis, The University of British Columbia, Vancouver, Canada.

1983d The Revival of Northwest Coast Indian Art. *In* Luke Rombout *et al., Vancouver: Art and Artists 1931-1983.* Vancouver: The Vancouver Art Gallery, pp 312-17.

Fenton, William N.

1960 The Museum and Anthropological Research. *Curator* 3(4): 327-335.

Freedman, Adele

1980 The Fellini of Fibreglass Thinks Big. *The Globe and Mail* Newspaper, Toronto, June 28, Entertainment p.3.

Freedman, Maurice

1978 *Main Trends in Social and Cultural Anthropology.* New York; Holmes and Meier.

Frese, H.H.

1960 *Anthropology and the Public: The Role of Museums.* Leiden: E.J. Brill.

Gardner, Helen

1959 *Art through the Ages.* New York: Harcourt Brace & Co., 4th edition.

Gibbons, Paul "Garbanzo"

1983 Summation...A Fool's Ransom — A Play in One Act. *In* Manning 1983: 321-331.

Graburn, Nelson H.H.

1968 Art and Acculturative Process. *International Social Science Journal* 21 (3): 457-68.

1976 *Ethnic and Tourist Arts: Cultural Expressions from the Fourth World.*

Berkeley and Los Angeles: University of California Press.

Green, Bryan R.

1977 On the Evaluation of Sociological Theory. *Philosophy of Social Sciences* 7: 33-50.

Guba, Egon G., and Y.S. Lincoln

1983 *Effective Evaluation,* San Franscisco: Jossey-Bass.

Guedon, Marie-Françoise

1983 A Case of Mistaken Identity (the Education of a Naive Museum Ethnologist). *In* Manning 1983a, pp. 253-261.

Hallowell, Christopher

1983 The Proper Study of Mankind. Nova: Anthropology on Trial, November 1. *The Dial* KCTS 9, Seattle, 4 (11), November, pp. 46-47.

Halpin, Marjorie M.

1978 Review of "The 12,000 Year Gap: Archaeology in British Columbia," and "First Peoples: Indian Cultures in British Columbia" at the British Columbia Provincial Museum. Canadian Museums Association *Gazette* 11 (1): 40-48.

1979 *Cycles: The Grapnic Art of Robert Davidson. Haida.* Vancouver: UBC Museum of Anthropology, Museum Note Number 7.

1983 Anthropology as Artefact. *In* Manning 1983a, pp. 262-275.

Harris, Neil

1981 *Humbug, The Art of P.T. Barnum.* Chicago: University of Chicago Press.

Harris, Marvin

1979 *Cultural Materialism: The Struggle for a Science of Culture.* New York: Random House.

Hawthorn, Audrey

1956 *People of the Potlatch: Native Arts & Culture of the Pacific Northwest Coast.* Vancouver: Evergreen Press Ltd.

Hoebel, E. Adamson, Richard Currier, and Susan Kaiser, eds.

1982 *Crisis in Anthropology: View from Spring Hill, 1980.* New York: Garland.

Holecek, Barbara G.

1983 Papua New Guinea: Anthropology of Trial. Boston: WGBH Transcripts.

Holm, Bill

1965 *Northwest Coast Indian Art: An Analysis of Form.* Seattle & London: University of Washington Press.

Hume, R.M.

1958 *One Hundred Years of B.C. Art: An Exhibition Held at the Vancouver Art Gallery to Commemorate the British Columbia Centennial Year.* Vancouver: Keystone Press Ltd.

Hymes, Dell

1969 The Use of Anthropology: Critical, Political, Personal, *In* Dell Hymes ed., *Reinventing Anthropology.* New York. Pantheon Books, pp. 3-82.

Illich, Ivan

1971 The De-Schooling of Society, *In* Bruce Rusk, ed., *Alternatives on Education.* Toronto: General Publishing Company, pp. 103-126.

Inglis, Stephen

1979 Cultural Readjustment: A Canadian Case Study. Canadian Museums Association *Gazette* 12 (3): 26-31.

1982 "Good Lord Man, This Stuff is Crude": Beneath the Patina of Canadian Folk Art. Paper presented to the Ninth Annual Conference of the Canadian Ethnology Society, Vancouver, Canada, May 9.

Johnson, Eve

1983 A Celebration of Art and Elegance. *The Sun* Newspaper, Vancouver, Canada, Thursday, Oct. 13, p. D1.

Kelly, Robert F.

1982 Museums As Status Symbols: A Cynic's View of Museum—Public Interface. Paper presented to the Ninth Annual Conference of the Canadian Ethnology Society, Vancouver, Canada, May 10.

1983 The Socio-symbolic Role of Museums. Paper presented to the XIth International Congress of Anthropological and Ethnological Sciences, Vancouver, August.

Key, Archie F.

1976 *Beyond Four Walls: The Origin and Development of Canadian*

Museums. Toronto: McClelland and Stewart.

Kopper, Philip

1982 *The National Museum of Natural History.* New York: Harry N. Abrams, Inc.

Lambert, Anne M.

1983 *Storage of Textiles and Costumes: Guidelines for Decision Making.* Vancouver: University of British Columbia Museum of Anthropology.

Lawless, Benjamin and Marilyn S. Cohen

1977 The Smithsonian style. In the Smithsonian Institutions, The Smithsonian Experience. Science-History-The Arts... The Treasures of the Nation. New York: W.W. Norton. Pp. 52-59.

Levine, Louis D., and Henry Sears.

1982 The ROM: No Disneyland. Letters to the Editor. *Maclean's Magazine,* Toronto, November 8, p. 10.

Levi-Strauss, C.

1843 The Art of the Northwest Coast at the American Museum of Natural History. *Gazette des Beaux-Arts* 24: 175-82.

Lewis, Brian N.

1980 The Museum as an Educational Facility. *Museum Journal* 80 (3): 151-155.

Loubser, Jan J.

1983 Consciousness, Inquiry, Imagination and Action. *In* Manning 1983a, pp. 12-21.

Lurie, Nancy Oestreich

1981 Museumland Revisited. *Human Organization* 40 (2): 180-187.

MacCannell, Dean

1976 *The Tourist: A New Theory of the Leisure Class.* New York: Schocken Books.

MacDonald, George F., et al.

1977 *Northwest Coast Indian Artists Guild: 1977 Graphics Collection* Ottawa: Canadian Indian Marketing Services.

Macfarlane, Nathalie, and Stephen Inglis

1977 *Norman Tait, Nishga Carver.* Vancouver: UBC Museum of Anthropology Museum Note Series.

Macfarlane, Nathalie

1978 *Joe David.* Vancouver: UBC Museum of Anthropology Museum Note Series.

MacGregor, Arthur

1983a Collectors and Collections of Rarities in the Sixteenth and Seventeenth Centuries. *In* MacGregor 1983b, pp. 70-97.

MacGregor, Arthur, ed.

1983b *Tradescant's Rarities. Essays on the Foundations of the Ashmolean Museum, 1683 with a Catalogue of the Surviving Early Collections.* Oxford: Clarendon Press.

McFeat, Tom F.S.

1962 Museum Ethnology and the Algonkian Project. *Anthropology Papers,* National Museums of Canada, No. 2.

McMartin, Pete

1983 A Gallery You Must See for Yourself. *The Sun* Newspaper, Vancouver, Wed. October 12, p. 5.

Malinowski, Bronislaw

1929 Practical Anthropology. *Africa* 2:22-38.

Manning, Frank

1983a *Consciousness and Inquiry: Ethnology and Canadian Realities.* Ottawa: National Museums of Canada.

1983b Confusion and Creative Engagement: a Comment on Canadian Ethnology. *In* Manning 1983a, pp. 2-11.

Mead, Margaret, and R.L. Bunzel, eds.

1960 *The Golden Age of American Anthropology.* New York: George Braziller.

Merton, Robert K.

1972 Insiders and Outsiders: a Chapter in the Sociology of Knowledge. *American Journal of Sociology* 78(1):9-47.

Meyer, Karl E.

1979 *The Art Museum, Power, Money, Ethics.* New York: Morrow.

Mitchell, John

1983 News Release: Briefing Notes on a Western Vancouver Island Cultural Enterprise. City of Port Alberni, British Columbia, Canada, March 5.

Morris, Brian

1983 The Special Demands Placed upon Museums by Their Users. Paper presented to the Thirteenth General Conference of the International Council of Museums, London, 23 July.

Nader, Laura

1969 Up the Anthropologist—Perspectives Gained from Studying Up. *In* Dell Hymes, ed., *Reinventing Anthropology.* New York: Pantheon, pp. 284-311.

1980 *No Access to Law.* New York: Academic Press.

1980 The Vertical Slice: Hierarchies and Children. *In* Gerald M. Britan and Ronald Cohen, eds., *Hierarchy and Society: Anthropological Perspectives on Bureaucracy.* Philadelphia: Institute for the Study of Human Issues, pp. 31-44.

1983 Who Reviews the Reviewers? *American Anthropologist* 85: 660-662.

Nason, James D.

1981 A Question of Patrimony: Ethical Issues in the Collecting of Cultural Objects. British Columbia Museum Association *Round-up*, No. 83, pp. 13-20.

National Museums of Canada

1982 Exhibitions Assistance Programmes and Museums of Human and Natural History, Science and Technology. Unpublished Manuscript, 2 pages.

Newton, Douglas

1981 The Art of Africa, the Pacific Islands, and the Americas. *The Metropolitan Museum of Art Bulletin.* Fall.

Parsons, T., and Gerald M. Platt

1973 *The American University.* Cambridge: Harvard University Press.

Preston, Richard J.

1983 The Social Structure of an Unorganised Society: Beyond Intentions and Peripheral Boasians. *In* Manning 1983a, pp. 286-305

Ridington, Robin

1979 Mirrors and Masks. *Parabola* 4 (4): 84-90.

Rowan, Madeline B.

1978 The Museum — School and Theatre. British Columbia Museums Association *Round-up* 72: 32-33.

Salisbury, Richard F.

1983 Applied Anthropology in Canada — Problems and Prospects. *In* Manning 1983a, pp. 192-200.

Scholte, Bob

1969 Toward a Reflexive and Critical Anthropology. *In* Dell Hymes, ed., *Reinventing Anthropology*. New York: Pantheon, pp. 430-458.

Scott, Andrew

1978 B.C.'s Great Art Bonanza. *The Sun* Newspaper, Vancouver, 21 July.

Shadbolt, Jack

1954 Has B.C. Betrayed Its Heritage of Art? *The Province* Newspaper, Vancouver, 6 November.

Shadbolt, Doris, et al.

1967 *Arts of the Raven: Master Works by the Northwest Coast Indians*. Vancouver: Vancouver Art Gallery.

Shadbolt, Doris

1974 *Bill Reid: A Retrospective Exhibition*. Vancouver: Vancouver Art Gallery.

Shelly, Henry C.

1911 *The British Museum — Its History and Treasures*. Boston: L.C. Page.

Shils, Edward

1981 *Tradition*. Chicago: University of Chicago Press.

Siminovitch, Louis

1979 *University Research in Jeopardy. The Threat of Declining Enrollment.* Hull: Canadian Government Publishing Centre.

Singer, Milton

1972 *When a Great Tradition Modernizes. An Anthropological Approach to Indian Civilization*. New York: Praeger.

1977 On the Symbolic and Historic Structure of an American Identity. *Ethos* 5 (4): 431-454.

Smithsonian Institution

1977 *The Smithsonian Experience. Science—History—The Arts...The Treasures of the Nation*. New York: Norton.

Special Committee on Antiquities

1959 Final Report of the Special Committee of Antiquities. Colombo: *Government of Ceylon Sessional Papers VII.*

Squires, Donald P.

1969 Schizophrenia: The Plight of the Natural History Curator. *Museum News* 48 (2): 18-21.

Stocking, George W., Jr.

1971 *Race, Culture, and Evolution: Essays in the History of Anthropology.* New York: The Free Press/Macmillan.

Sturtevant, William C.

1969 Does Anthropology Need Museums? *Proceedings of the Biological Society of Washington* 182: 619-650.

Taylor, William E. Jr., et al.

1978 *Northwest Coast Indian Artists Guild 1978 Graphics Collection.* Ottawa: Canadian Indian Marketing Services.

1982 *Sharing the Challenge: An Invitation to Comment on New Public Facilities for the National Museum of Man.* Ottawa: National Museum of Man.

Tremblay, Marc-Adélard

1983 Anthropology in Question: What Knowledge and Knowledge for What? *In* Manning 1983a, pp. 332-347.

Vallance, Julie

1981 *The Internal Dynamics of the Community Museum.* Unpublished M.A. thesis, the University of British Columbia, Vancouver, Canada.

Vastokas, Joan M.

1975 Bill Reid and the Native Renaissance. *artscanada,* June, Numbers 198/9.

Wallace, Irving

1959 *The Fabulous Showman. The Life and Times of P.T. Barnum.* New York: Signet Books from New American Library and Alfred A. Knopf.

Washburn, Wilcomb E.

1961 Scholarship and the Museum. *Museum News,* October, pp. 16-19.

1969 Are Museums Necessary? *Museum News,* October.

Weaver, Sally M.

1981 *Making Canadian Indian Policy. The Hidden Agenda 1968-1979.* Toronto: University of Toronto Press.

Welch, Martin

1983 The Ashmolean as Described by its Earliest Visitors. *In* MacGregor 1983b, pp. 59-69.

Wilson, Thomas

1891 Anthropology at the Paris Exposition in 1889. *Annual Report of the Smithsonian Institution for 1890.* Washington, pp. 654-680.

Wolf, Robert L.

1980 A Naturalistic View of Evaluation. *Museum News,* July/August, pp 39-45.

Young, David R.

1980 *Northwest Renaissance.* Burnaby, B.C.. The Burnaby Art Gallery.

Index